970.1 HUN
Hunt.

D1072374

SPEEDWAY PUBLIC LIBRARY
SPEEDWAY, INDIANA

970.1 HUN
Hunt.

AMERICAN INDIAN
SURVIVAL SKILLS

SPEEDWAY PUBLIC LIBRARY
SPEEDWAY, INDIANA

Bull Dance, Mandan-O-kee-pa ceremony, George Catlin, 1832.
Photograph courtesy of Smithsonian Institution, National Museum of
the American Indian.

AMERICAN INDIAN
SURVIVAL SKILLS

W. BEN HUNT

Outdoor
Life®
Books

Meredith® Press
New York

Adapted from The Complete How-To Book of Indiancraft

To my wife, Laura, without whose patience, tolerance and interest this book would not have materialized.

Published by:
  Outdoor Life® Books
  Meredith® Press
  150 East 52nd Street
  New York, New York 10022

Distributed by the Meredith Corporation, Des Moines, Iowa

For Meredith® Press:
Director: Elizabeth P. Rice
Assistant: Ruth Weadock
Executive Editor: Connie Schrader
Editorial Assistant: Carolyn Mitchell
Production Manager: Bill Rose
Designer: Ulrich Ruchti

Brief quotation may be used in critical articles and review. For any other reproduction of the book, however, including electronic, mechanical, photocopying, recording, or other means, written permission must be obtained from the publisher.

Copyright © 1973 by Macmillan Publishing Company, a Division of Macmillan, Inc.
Copyright © 1991 by Meredith® Press

This edition is adapted by arrangement with Macmillan Publishing Company, a Division of Macmillan, Inc. from THE COMPLETE HOW-TO BOOK OF INDIANCRAFT by W. Ben Hunt. Copyright © 1973 by Macmillan Publishing Company.

Distributed by the Meredith Corporation, Des Moines, Iowa
ISBN: 0-696-11121-7
Library of Congress Catalog Card Number: 91-052552

Printed in the United States of America

10 9 8 7 6 5 4 3 2 1

Before starting any project, study the diagrams carefully, read and observe all safety precautions provided by any tool or equipment manufacturer and follow all generally accepted safety procedures.

060712

EDITOR'S INTRODUCTION

W. Ben Hunt was born in Wisconsin over a hundred years ago. Most of his life was spent in teaching, art work, writings and lecturing about Indiancraft and campcraft. He was a self-taught expert on the crafts of the Plains and Woodland Indians, and he spent several years traveling in the Southwest to acquaint himself with the techniques of silverwork that are part of the Navajo and Hopi tradition.

American Indian Survival Skills is compiled from several books that were published in the late 1930's and early 1940's. We have tried to collect the most usable and amusing projects and assemble them in a logical and clear organization.

Although most of us will probably never be forced to use our own hands, wits, and woodcraft to survive on a camping trip or in the woods, a knowledge of such skills is invaluable. Everyone should be able to use a knife, ax, or thongs, to make simple tools and equipment. And, being able to survive using your own Indian woodcraft skills makes you feel so confident it is worth collecting the knowledge.

Many of the authentic methods for making things that are shown in this book are not known by younger Indians. Much of the information has been obtained through interviews with "old-timers," and through careful research into Indian folklore and skin paintings.

SPEEDWAY PUBLIC LIBRARY
SPEEDWAY, INDIANA

For example, the weaving of the beautiful woodland Indian bags is an art that has almost disappeared.

When using this book, try to think like the Indian. Select what you can from nature, adapt it for your own use, make your own tools, and always be aware of the bounty of materials that is part of the American Indian heritage. Give thanks for the saplings, the rough leather thongs, and the colorful nature-inspired designs. In using the techniques of woodcraft and campcraft of the American Indian, you are fashioning objects that re-create the time and life of a great people. But, most of all, enjoy the forests, and live for and with the land that the Indians loved so well.

This edition of W. Ben Hunt's work was created with the help of two wonderful researchers: Susan Otto of the Milwaukee Public Museum Photo Collection in Milwaukee, Wisconsin, and Laura Nash of the Museum of the American Indian in New York City. Laura Nash allowed the editors and designer to visit the museum, and helped access photographs that seemed to reflect the projects in W. Ben Hunt's illustrations. Susan Otto sent us dozens of photocopies of artifacts and helped us select from her extensive files. This work is time consuming, and we appreciate the extra effort that was made.

CONTENTS

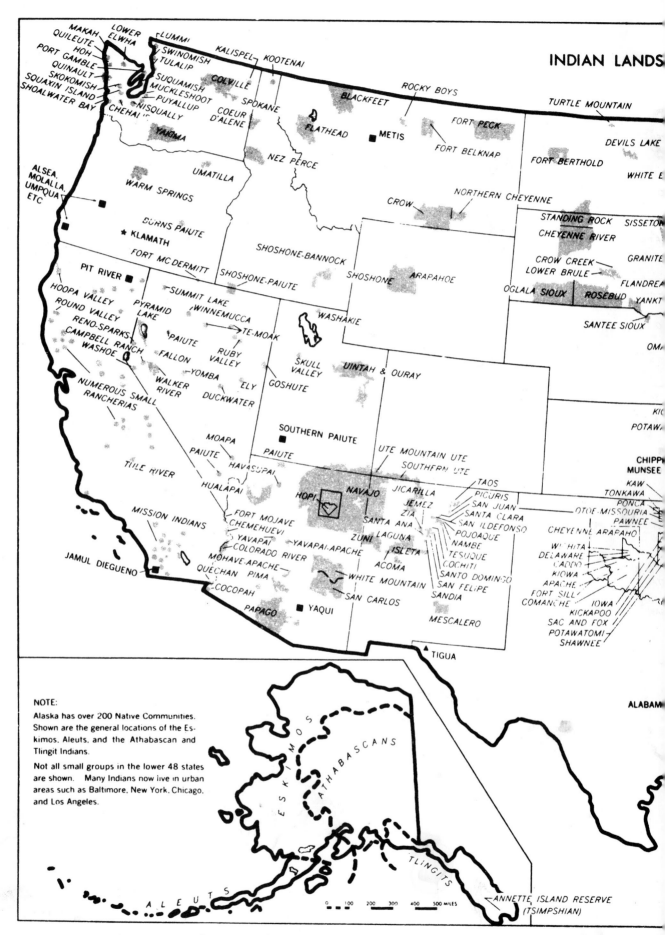

INDIAN LANDS

MAKAH
QUILEUTE
HOH
PORT GAMBLE
QUINAULT
SKOKOMISH
SQUAXIN ISLAND
SHOALWATER BAY
LOWER ELWHA
LUMMI
SWINOMISH
TULALIP
KALISPEL
KOOTENAI
SUQUAMISH
MUCKLESHOOT
PUYALLUP
NISQUALLY
CHEHALIS
COLVILLE
SPOKANE
COEUR D'ALENE
YAKIMA
ROCKY BOYS
BLACKFEET
TURTLE MOUNTAIN
FLATHEAD
METIS
FORT PECK
FORT BELKNAP
DEVILS LAKE
FORT BERTHOLD
WHITE E
NEZ PERCE
UMATILLA
ALSEA, MOLALLA, UMPQUA, ETC
WARM SPRINGS
BURNS PAIUTE
KLAMATH
FORT MC DERMITT
NORTHERN CHEYENNE
CROW
STANDING ROCK
SISSETON
CHEYENNE RIVER
CROW CREEK
LOWER BRULE
GRANITE
FLANDREA
OGLALA SIOUX
ROSEBUD
YANKT
SANTEE SIOUX
OM
PIT RIVER
SHOSHONE-BANNOCK
SHOSHONE-PAIUTE
SHOSHONE
ARAPAHOE
HOOPA VALLEY
ROUND VALLEY
RENO-SPARKS
CAMPBELL RANCH
WASHOE
SUMMIT LAKE
WINNEMUCCA
PYRAMID LAKE
PAIUTE
TE-MOAK
WASHAKIE
FALLON
RUBY VALLEY
YOMBA
WALKER RIVER
ELY
DUCKWATER
GOSHUTE
SKULL VALLEY
UINTAH & OURAY
NUMEROUS SMALL RANCHERIAS
MOAPA
PAIUTE
PAIUTE
HAVASUPAI
SOUTHERN PAIUTE
UTE MOUNTAIN UTE
SOUTHERN UTE
TAOS
TULE RIVER
HUALAPAI
HOPI
NAVAJO
JICARILLA
PICURIS
SAN JUAN
SANTA CLARA
SAN ILDEFONSO
POJOAQUE
NAMBE
TESUQUE
COCHITI
SANTO DOMINGO
SAN FELIPE
SANDIA
MESCALERO
JEMEZ
ZIA
SANTA ANA
LAGUNA
ISLETA
ACOMA
ZUNI
CHIPP
MUNSEE
KAW
TONKAWA
PONCA
OTOE-MISSOURIA
PAWNEE
CHEYENNE ARAPAHO
WICHITA
DELAWARE
CADDO
KIOWA
APACHE
FORT SILL
COMANCHE
IOWA
KICKAPOO
SAC AND FOX
POTAWATOMI
SHAWNEE
KIO
POTAW
MISSION INDIANS
FORT MOJAVE
CHEMEHUEVI
YAVAPAI
COLORADO RIVER
MOHAVE-APACHE
QUECHAN
COCOPAH
PIMA
YAVAPAI-APACHE
WHITE MOUNTAIN
SAN CARLOS
JAMUL DIEGUENO
PAPAGO
YAQUI
TIGUA
ALABAM

NOTE:

Alaska has over 200 Native Communities. Shown are the general locations of the Eskimos, Aleuts, and the Athabascan and Tlingit Indians.

Not all small groups in the lower 48 states are shown. Many Indians now live in urban areas such as Baltimore, New York, Chicago, and Los Angeles.

ESKIMOS
ATHABASCANS
TLINGITS
ALEUTS
ANNETTE ISLAND RESERVE
(TSIMPSHIAN)

0   100   200   300   400   500 MILES

COMMUNITIES

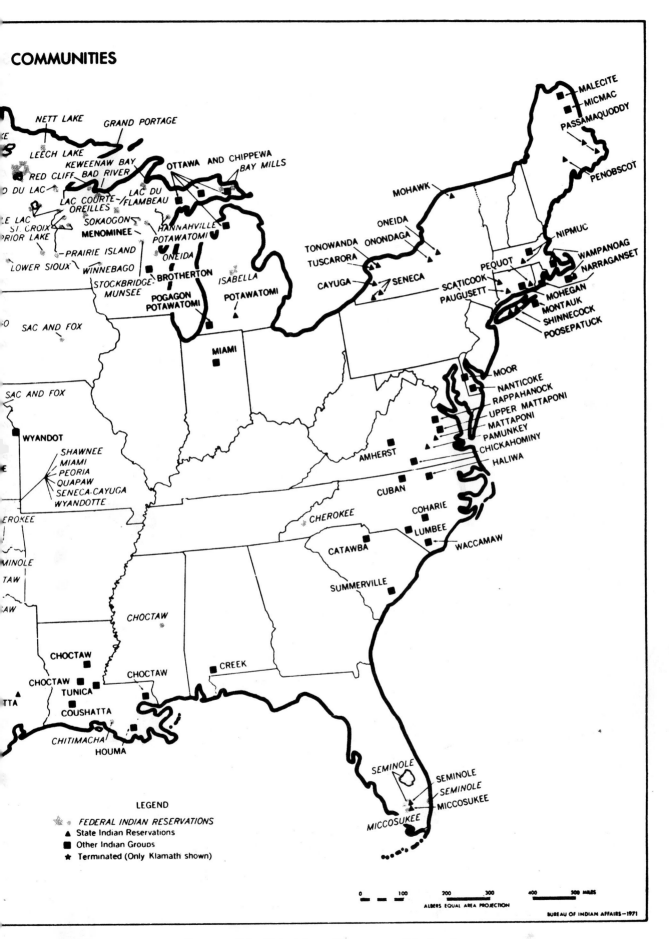

NETT LAKE GRAND PORTAGE
LEECH LAKE
KEWEENAW BAY OTTAWA AND CHIPPEWA
RED CLIFF BAD RIVER BAY MILLS
D DU LAC
LAC COURTE~ LAC DU
OREILLES FLAMBEAU
SOKAOGON HANNAHVILLE
E LAC
ST CROIX MENOMINEE POTAWATOMI
PRIOR LAKE
PRAIRIE ISLAND ONEIDA
LOWER SIOUX WINNEBAGO
STOCKBRIDGE- BROTHERTON ISABELLA
MUNSEE POGAGON
POTAWATOMI POTAWATOMI

MALECITE
MICMAC
PASSAMAQUODDY

PENOBSCOT

MOHAWK

ONEIDA
TONOWANDA ONONDAGA
TUSCARORA
CAYUGA SENECA

NIPMUC

WAMPANOAG
PEQUOT NARRAGANSET
SCATICOOK
PAUGUSETT MOHEGAN
MONTAUK
SHINNECOCK
POOSEPATUCK

SAC AND FOX

MIAMI

MOOR
NANTICOKE
RAPPAHANOCK
UPPER MATTAPONI
MATTAPONI
PAMUNKEY
CHICKAHOMINY
HALIWA

SAC AND FOX
WYANDOT
SHAWNEE
MIAMI
PEORIA
QUAPAW
SENECA-CAYUGA
WYANDOTTE

AMHERST

CUBAN

EROKEE

CHEROKEE

COHARIE
LUMBEE
WACCAMAW

CATAWBA

SUMMERVILLE

INOLE
TAW

CHOCTAW

CHOCTAW

CHOCTAW

CHOCTAW CREEK
CHOCTAW
TUNICA
TTA
COUSHATTA
CHITIMACHA
HOUMA

SEMINOLE
SEMINOLE
SEMINOLE
MICCOSUKEE
MICCOSUKEE

LEGEND

FEDERAL INDIAN RESERVATIONS
▲ State Indian Reservations
■ Other Indian Groups
★ Terminated (Only Klamath shown)

0   100   200   300   400   500 MILES
ALBERS EQUAL AREA PROJECTION

BUREAU OF INDIAN AFFAIRS—1971

Courtesy of the United States Department of the Interior.

AN INTRODUCTION TO INDIAN SURVIVAL SKILLS

It may be well to mention that it is not necessary to follow the instructions accompanying each plate to the last detail. Other materials than those mentioned may serve just as well. If, for instance, no rawhide is available for thongs, the so-called rawhide or pigskin lacing may be used, as well as good heavy cord—waxed if necessary—or soft copper wire, the ends of which are twisted and bent down so as not to scratch. The tom-tom, for example, may be made of some other leather. Its tone may not be the same as that of one made with rawhide, but it will sound fairly well and will look equally well after it has been decorated.

The directions given for soaking or stretching the rawhide must, however, be followed also for the substituted leather. Then, too, while the projects are proportioned correctly, there are times when the materials at hand will not permit making them the exact size or shape shown. In such cases the designs may, of course, be altered, using the drawings as a basis.

The Indian worked with the things he had on hand. Years ago, he decorated birch-bark baskets and many other articles with dyed porcupine quills. At that time these quills were easy to get. Now beads are cheap and can be more easily obtained. Beads consequently are used more often than quills. Today, tepees are no longer made of skins sewed together, but of canvas. Leggings that were at one time made of soft buckskin are now mostly made of blanket cloth or other· material that may be on hand or obtained easily.

As soon as the white man brought iron to this country, the Indian made use of it for arrowheads, knives, and tomahawks. The stone and flint, which he had previously used for these purposes, were discarded. Therefore, use the material on hand and substitute it for the material that is specified. Watercolor paints are just as bright and beautiful as those prepared with oil. However, if water colors are used they should be lacquered or varnished to protect them against moisture. If beads are not available for decorating, paint the designs on the wood or leather or cloth with glossy enamel or lacquer. A brightly decorated buckskin vest at a recent powwow proved, upon closer inspection to have painted instead of beaded decorations.

W. BEN HUNT

BASIC TOOLS AND MATERIALS

The Workshop

Probably the most expensive piece of equipment is the workbench. It should be quite rigid and strong enough to hold a 3- or 4-inch vise. A few shelves and tool racks to keep materials and tools complete the home workshop. As more and more things are added, they are gradually placed in the most convenient places. Cupboards with glass doors may be built to keep things where they won't get dusty.

Industrial arts shops at schools and community colleges are sometimes available and may be used for doing the kind of work described in this book. Here, too, a place must be provided where finished and

Fig. 1. An open-air shop.

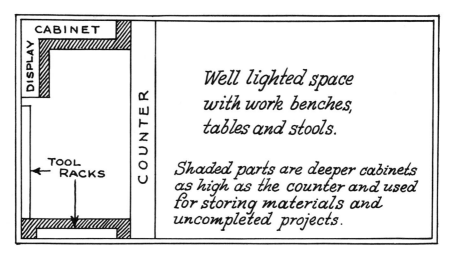

Fig. 2 Plan of an open-air shop.

unfinished work may be stored so that it will not be handled by everyone. Cupboards are the best solution for that problem. There should also be places for storing materials like leather, feathers, raffia, and the like. These storage cases should be locked.

Lights for handicraft work should be bright and not too high. Lights placed 3 or 4 feet from the work are better than those placed near the ceiling. All lights should be equipped with metal reflectors.

At hunter's camps, a cabin of some sort is usually set aside to be used as a workshop. This should be furnished with tables and benches placed where the light is good. There should also be cupboards and lockers for the tools and materials, and a place to display finished articles. There should be a place for every tool, and each place should be marked with a silhouette of that tool. In this way, a glance at the tool rack will tell which tools are missing. A counter of some sort across one end of the room which sets that end of the room apart as a tool and storage room is another method of keeping things in order.

Unless a cabin or building is well ventilated, it is not an ideal workshop in the warm weather, and for that reason an airy place should be provided for hot days. Sometimes a few benches in a shady place will be sufficient; but where there are several workers, a more elaborate area must be worked out. An ideal open-air shop can be built somewhat like a picnic booth (see Figures 1 and 2) with the counters built about 28 inches above the ground so that you can sit while they are working.

If this open-air shop is built in the woods away from other buildings, provisions must be made to store materials and tools. Naturally, these should be kept where wind and rain will not harm them. It would be ideal if a small cabin or shed could be built at one end of the shop where all tools, materials, and unfinished projects could be safely stored. A shop of this kind can be built with a framework of small logs, if they are available; this, in itself, would be a worthwhile project.

Besides workbenches, there should be benches to sit on while working. These may be made of lumber or slabs, and will be useful as seating at other times. The size of the open-air shop is, of course, determined by the number of people using it.

In windy places some sort of protection should be provided for those working with light materials. Where the sun beats down all day, or where it rains frequently, the roof should project out beyond the benches for both shade and shelter.

Tools

Most of the projects illustrated in this book may be made with nothing more than an ax and a pocketknife. It is not necessary, however, to limit yourself in the matter of tools, if they are on hand. Everything shown in this book can be made with the tools in the following list:

ripsaw
crosscut saw
hand ax
pocket knife
brace
auger bits and drills
chisel and gouges
Carborundum wheel
   (hand or motor driven)
oil or Carborundum
   whetstone
thin lubricating oil

leather punch
   (a nail may do)
leather and beading
   needles
small paint brushes
vise and clamps
files
block plane
drawknife
spokeshave
hammer
awl

Many of these tools are found in most homes. To be of real service, tools should be kept in good condition. For this reason, the whetstone is a necessary item. It is not only easier but safer to cut with sharp rather than dull tools.

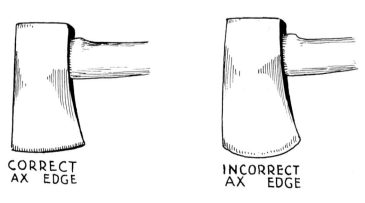

CORRECT
AX EDGE

INCORRECT
AX EDGE

Fig. 3

Fig. 4

Saws used for cutting green wood should have more set than those for ordinary use, because, after the cut has been started, the saw will stick or bind due to the swelling of the wood.

A small hand ax will serve the purpose for all of the work shown. Such an ax should be sharpened so that its edge is shaped like the one shown in Figure 3. Axes that are rounded like the one shown in Figure 4 may slip toward the user and cause injury.

While some people may be able to carve with a camp knife, it is best to use that knife for carving meat and to get a pocketknife like the one shown in Figure 5 for real work. Get one with two or three blades, one 2½-inches long for heavy work, and one or two small blades, each about 1½-inches long for fine work. It pays to get a good knife as it will keep an edge. A knife will get dull with use, but one blade should always be kept razor sharp for the time when it is really needed. Knives equipped with rings and chains are not really handy. It is better to get into the habit of closing your knife and putting the knife into your pocket after each use.

A brace and a set of bits and a few small drills come in handy, especially when green basswood is being

Fig. 5

used, but holes may be bored with a pocketknife. Indians and woodsmen frequently use a red-hot iron to burn holes into wood when no bit and brace is available.

Files, chisels, and gouges are always useful and, if possible, should be in the tool chest; there should also be a plane or two.

A Carborundum wheel is a useful tool to have around, especially if you must grind a chip or a nick out of an ax or a chisel. A hand wheel will serve; and even with such a wheel, be careful not to burn the tool that is being sharpened.

A vise and a few wood clamps will frequently prove helpful. When necessary, a wood or a C-clamp may be used as a vise.

While an awl can be easily and quickly made with a piece of wood, a nail, and a file—an awl of good steel is best. Ice picks usually serve very well, too. Try carving out fine awl handles like those shown in Figure 6. Carving these handles is a good pastime, and the material out of which they are made may be carried in your pocket and whittled during spare moments.

Although you can get along without a drawknife or

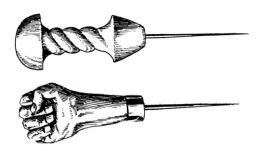

Fig. 6

a spokeshave, they are timesavers. They should be kept very sharp, or they will split the wood instead of cutting it.

Needles are important for leather sewing (see Figure 7). Leather needles are like ordinary needles but they have blunt points. This makes it easier to follow the holes made with a punch. Glover's needles are sharp and will force or cut their way through thin leather, due to sharp edges. To use them, you should have a good thimble with which to push them through. Beading needles must be very thin in order that they and the thread may be passed twice through the hole of the bead. These needles are used only for loom beading.

Fig. 7

Materials

It is often difficult to find the material you want to use. As was mentioned before, you should use what material is on hand, if possible. For example, the Hopi dolls may be whittled out of any softwood that can be found along the roadsides or in the woods. Check with the owner of the property before cutting, whether the wood is along the road or in woods or pastures. When saplings are cut, the ends should be painted or shellacked to prevent them from checking and then splitting. When saplings are required for any of the projects that necessitate bending, do not cut them until you are ready to use them. If that is not possible, keep the saplings moist by tying them in a bundle and placing them in a creek or lake, and weigh them down with a few flat stones. If it is impossible to place them in water, they may be wrapped in wet gunny sacks and kept in a shady place. This will keep them in condition so that they may be easily bent.

Oxbows, like the ones shown on the yoke in Figure 8, must be very strong. They are, therefore, made of hickory or other equally tough saplings from 1- to 2-inches in diameter and are bent while green. It is a rather slow process, but the life is not taken out of the wood as it would be by steaming. Besides, the farmers

Fig. 8

who still make them have no steaming tanks to handle a 5-foot piece of wood. Another point in favor of using green saplings is the fact that you are assured of straight grain. The wood for most of the projects described in this series will bend quite easily if a little care and time are taken. A week or two of drying will be enough to give the pieces the required set.

The Indians used smoke-tanned buckskin for their moccasins. This is getting scarce, but chrome-tanned buckskin may be substituted and will serve quite well, except that it will not withstand wetting like the smoke-tanned variety. Split cowhide, like that used for glove leather, may be purchased from tanneries or leather goods companies, and will serve very well for moccasins. When buying leather, state what it is to be used for, and the color wanted. Gray, yellow, or cream are the best colors for moccasins.

For those who have the facilities for preparing rawhide, we have furnished a plate on that subject. It is quite simple to do and need not be a smelly job at all, provided that the scraps of flesh and hair are cleaned up. Rawhide may be prepared in a basement, without anyone being bothered by the odor.

For those who do not want to do this, there are a few places where thin rawhide may be obtained, but it is expensive. Unless you know a tannery where it is manufactured, it must be bought from a firm using it in some manufacturing process. Some luggage companies use rawhide for handles and straps.

Feathers are often hard to get. Those living in rural sections may get them from farmers or poultry raisers.

Large hacksaw blades used for knifes can frequently be obtained for the asking at machine shops, where the blades, when dull, are usually thrown away.

W. Ben Hunt

HOW TO MAKE RAWHIDE

Although the plate on the opposite page contains all that is essential for preparing rawhide, a few more explanatory words may assist the beginner.

In the first place, get the smallest calfskin obtainable. Thick rawhide is hard to work; besides, thin rawhide is much better, especially for lacing. Where strength is needed, the lacing may be doubled.

Preparing rawhide is not necessarily a smelly job. If the hide is dehaired as soon as the hair becomes loose, and if the hide is not allowed to stay wet too long, there should be no disagreeable odor at all. The scrapings and hair should be burned or buried when the job is finished.

Rawhide has many uses. It shrinks when dry, holding whatever is tied with it more firmly and yet more flexibly than rope or wire. When lacings are kept dry, joints bound with them will remain tight. For this reason, protect them with a good coat of varnish.

The French Canadians use rawhide for weaving chair seats. The timbers of the Mormon Tabernacle in Salt Lake City are bound together with heavy rawhide thongs. Indians made their saddle frames of bone and horn laced together with rawhide. They then covered the entire frame with rawhide sewed in place while wet.

A Few Uses for Rawhide

Tom-tom heads

Snowshoe lacing

Parfleches

Sandals

Western Indian moccasin
soles

Stone ax handle fastenings

Knife handles

Sled lashings

Chair seats

Indian saddle covers

Rattles

Lashing for crooked
knives

Hammer stick covers

Knife sheaths

Ax sheaths

Indian quirts

Woman decorating hide; Crow. Photograph courtesy of Smithsonian Institution, National Museum of the American Indian.

HOW TO MAKE RAWHIDE

1 Get a fresh green calf skin from your local butcher or slaughter house.

2 Trim off surplus flesh and fat with a sharp knife being careful not to cut into the skin.

3 Lay the skin, hair side up on a clean surface and sprinkle about an inch of clean, dry wood ash over the entire hair side.

4 Work it well into the hair.

5 Wet the ashes by sprinkling with rain water or water from a creek or lake, working the paste thus formed into the hair.

6 Fold hide with hair side in and roll into tight bundle. Tie with rope.

7 Place it in a hole in moist earth and cover with earth to keep outer portions from becoming dry, OR wrap it in wet burlap and place it where it can be kept moist.

8 Either way - it should lie for two or three days or until hair become loose.

SCRAPER MADE FROM TABLE-KNIFE BLADE DRIVEN INTO A PIECE OF WOOD. DRIVE NAILS THRU WOOD WHERE SHOWN AND CLINCH ON OTHER SIDE TO PREVENT WOOD FROM SPLITTING.

A BEAM IS SIMPLY A SMOOTH PEELED LOG OR HALF A LOG SET IN THE GROUND AT ABOUT THE ANGLE SHOWN HERE. THE UPPER END SHOULD BE ABOUT WAIST HIGH. BEAM SHOULD BE ABOUT 7" OR 8" WIDE. IF NO LOG IS AVAILABLE, ROUND OFF A PIECE OF 2"X 8" PLANK. THE WORKER PRESSES AGAINST HIDE TO KEEP IT FROM SLIPPING AND SHOULD WEAR WATERPROOF APRON.

SANDPAPER BLOCK OR PUMICE STONE USED TO SMOOTH DOWN RAWHIDE

9 Unroll the hide and rinse it thoroughly in soft water.

10 Scrape off the flesh side with scraper on beam as shown above.

11 Turn hide and scrape off the hair and the scarf skin at the same time, being careful not to cut into the hide. The motion is just the opposite from using a drawknife and calls for a little "elbow grease".

12 Rinse hide again in clear soft water and wring out as much water as possible by twisting.

13 Stretch hide as tight as possible and keep taking up the slack until hide is as tight as a drum.

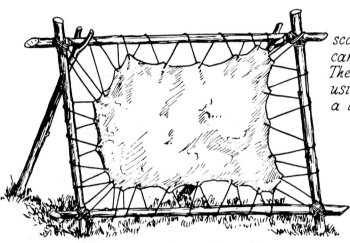

A DRYING FRAME MAY BE MADE OF SAPLINGS OR ANY OTHER WOOD STRONG ENOUGH TO WITHSTAND A GOOD PULL. ANY ¼" ROPE WILL DO FOR STRETCHING.

14 Set the stretcher and skin in a shady place where the air can circulate around it and allow it to become bone dry. You now have rawhide, but –

15 To really finish the job right, lay the hide on a smooth surface and go over both sides with a sandpaper block or a flat piece of pumice or sand stone. This smooths down any rough spots and also gives the rawhide a nice even texture.

16 Keep rawhide in a dry place. When ready to use, cut off as much as is needed and trim to size. Then soak it from 10 to 20 hours or until it is soft and pliable. Work it while it is wet, stretching it as much as possible, and when it dries it will be as tight and hard as a piece of sheet iron.

Plate on making tom-toms shows how rawhide lacings are cut.

Shellac or spar varnish will keep moisture out of finished work.

KNIFE AND AX SHEATHS

On the plates are shown sheaths for hunting or camp knives and for hand axes. Sheaths should be made to protect any knife of the rigid-blade type, such as sloyd knives, hunting knives, wood-carving knives, leather-skinning knives, and also for awls. This is to protect the edges and points from being dulled and also to protect oneself, especially when knives are thrown into a bag or box with a lot of other things. Sheaths for sloyd knives, awls, and the like, do not require a belt fastening as they are not carried around. They should fit snugly into their sheath, so that friction holds them in place. The sheaths may be made of wood and covered with leather or with regular friction tape. (See Figure 9). A sheath for an awl may be made of a piece of wood with a hole drilled into it, or of two pieces of leather sewed together.

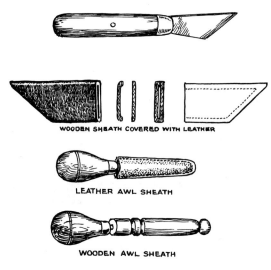

WOODEN SHEATH COVERED WITH LEATHER

LEATHER AWL SHEATH

WOODEN AWL SHEATH

Fig. 9

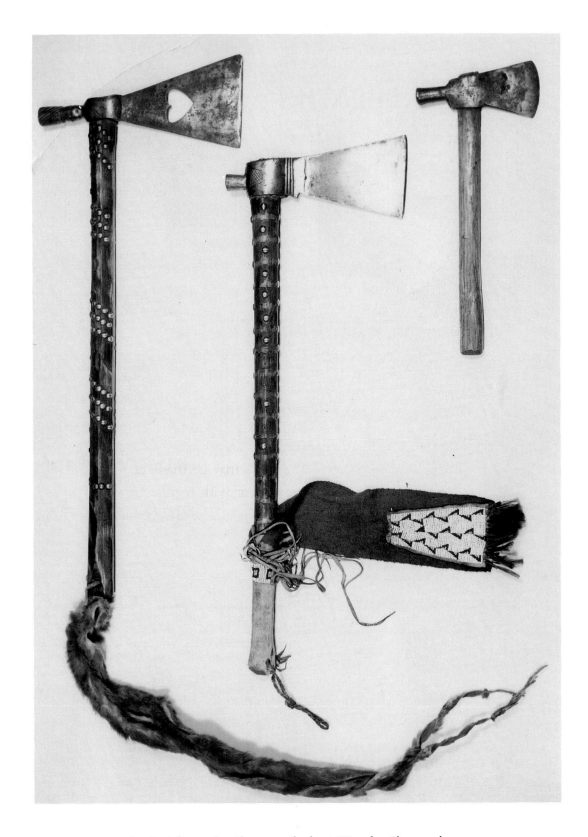

Tomahawks, left to right; Chippewa, Shoshoni, Wyandot. Photograph courtesy of Smithsonian Institution, National Museum of the American Indian.

KNIFE SHEATHS

Sheaths should be made of rather stiff leather. Cowhide or thick calf skin is best, and should be about 1/16 inch thick. For lacing use thin leather shoe laces, or cut it of thin leather about 1/8 inch wide. Use a leather punch if you have one or make one by filing off the end of an 8 or 10 penny nail depending on the size of the lacing. Lacing should fit snugly into the holes.

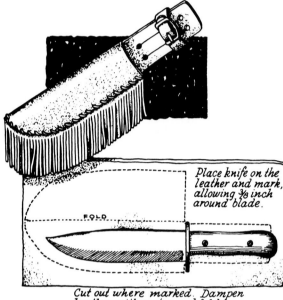

Place knife on the leather and mark, allowing 3/8 inch around blade.

FOLD

Cut out where marked. Dampen leather with water and fold.

Punch made of a nail

Punch holes 1/4 inch apart and 1/8 inch from the edge, punching thru both edges at the same time. Punch & cut slots for belt loop.

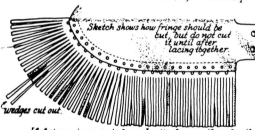

Sketch shows how fringe should be cut, but do not cut it until after lacing together.

wedges cut out.

3/8"

If fringe is wanted, make it of some thin leather and punch it as shown using one side of the sheath as template.

Lace as shown in upper sketch.

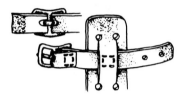

Fasten small strap with buckle as shown. Either sew it with waxed linen thread or punch & lace it with thin leather lacing.

If no fringe is wanted, treat edge as shown on ax sheath.

INDIAN TYPE

Make an inner sheath of leather or rawhide similar to the above sheath, but make it only as long as the blade. Then make an outer sheath of buckskin to go within an inch of the end of the handle. Bead partly or all over. Thongs "AA" are used to tie around the handle and "BB" are of thicker leather and are tied around the waist.

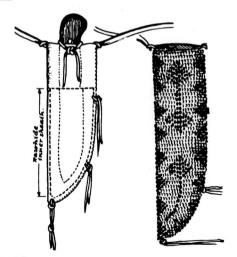

rawhide inner sheath.

AX SHEATHS

OPEN-TOP SHEATH

Back view of sheath completed.

Sew strap in place (before lacing the sheath) with waxed linen thread or fasten with thin leather lacing.

Place ax on the leather and mark pattern, allowing about ½ inch on lower edge and sides.

A

Allow for back of ax head.

Cut a piece of the same leather ⅜ inch wide to fit as shown. "A"

Sketch at top of page shows how strap is used to hold the ax in the sheath.

After strap is sewed in place, fold leather to proper shape & bring the strap over to locate slot in front.

Fold and punch thru both sides as shown below. Allow for handle

Punch and cut slots for belt loop.

A

Then put strip "A" in place on one half of sheath. Mark holes and punch them, or punch thru the holes in the sheath.

A

Strip "A" prevents ax or knife from cutting the lacing.

CLOSED-TOP SHEATH

Perhaps it would be well to make a paper pattern first to make sure that everything fits correctly.

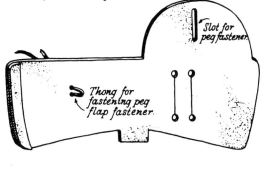

Slot for peg fastener

Thong for fastening peg flap fastener.

Use the same method of laying out this sheath as the one above, allowing ½ inch for play and lacing, and lace it the same way.

A good snap fastener may be used to lock the flap but a more woodsmanlike method would be as shown here.

Whittle peg of hardwood and make it a little shorter than the slot. Fasten with a piece of thin lacing.

31

SANDALS

Sandals have been used for hundreds of years and are still used in many countries today. Rawhide sandals may be used in dry climates only; they get quite slippery when wet. For an all around sandal, cowhide, canvas, or canvas-and-rubber belting is best. This latter material may be bought at any store handling machine or farm equipment. Canvas, and canvas-and-rubber belting are best suited for wet weather or around lakes and rivers since they will not warp or shrink when drying. However, the leather cross and tie straps must be kept pliable, or else they should be made of heavy tape or webbing such as is used for skate straps. Be sure to cut the sandals large enough. Be sure they are long enough to protect the heel and the toes.

Wolf mask with life-sized bearskin costume: wood and copper eyes, and upper teeth and haliotis shell, moveable jaw; Kwakiutl. Photograph courtesy of Milwaukee Public Museum.

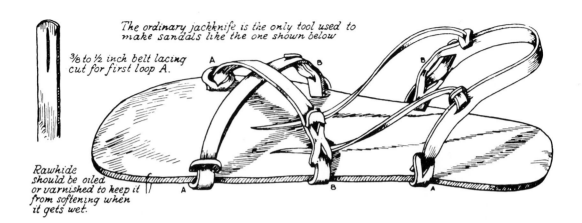

The ordinary jackknife is the only tool used to
make sandals like the one shown below

⅜ to ½ inch belt lacing
cut for first loop A.

A   B   B

Rawhide
should be oiled
or varnished to keep it
from softening when
it gets wet.

A   B   A

SANDALS
OF RAWHIDE OR COWHIDE

The first choice of leather for sandals is rawhide, if it is
obtainable. The next is cowhide, but any heavy
leather may be used. Leather or heavy canvas belting
also makes good sandals. The Mexican peons use old
auto tires for their sandals in this modern age. In some
countries sandals are made of braided or woven straw.
They may also be made of rope. Leather sandals should be
oiled to keep them pliable. The leather for the straps
should be rather
flexible so as not
to chafe the feet.

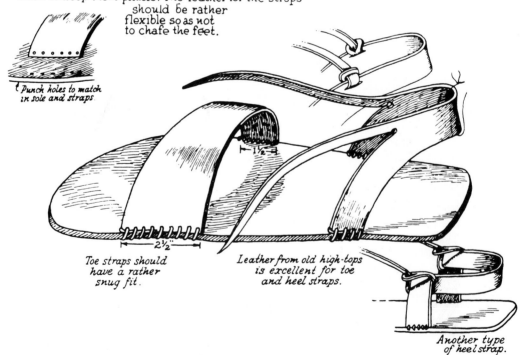

Punch holes to match
in sole and straps.

1½"

2½"

Toe straps should
have a rather
snug fit.

Leather from old high-tops
is excellent for toe
and heel straps.

Another type
of heel strap.

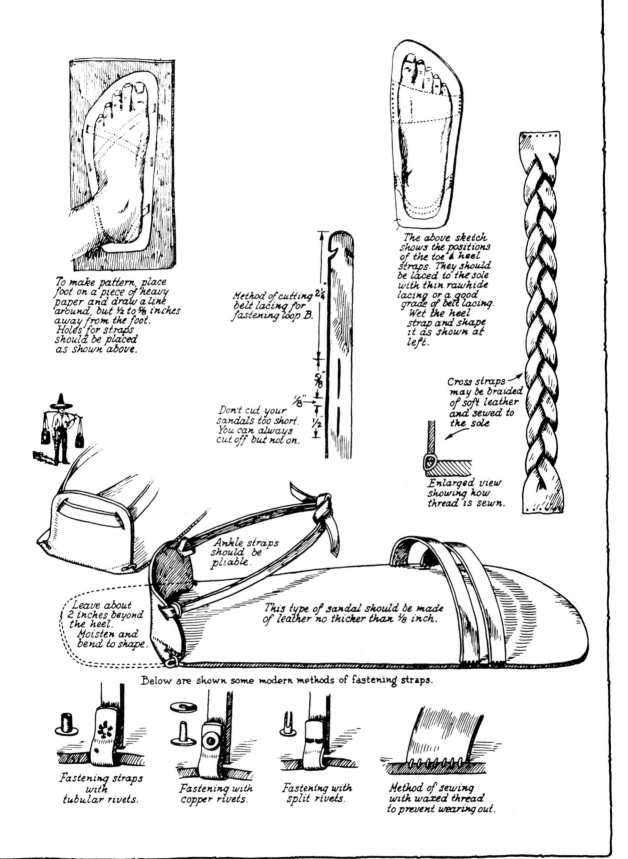

To make pattern, place foot on a piece of heavy paper and draw a line around, but ½ to ⅝ inches away from the foot. Holes for straps should be placed as shown above.

Method of cutting belt lacing for fastening loop B.

2⅜

⅝"

⅛"

½"

Don't cut your sandals too short. You can always cut off but not on.

The above sketch shows the positions of the toe & heel straps. They should be laced to the sole with thin rawhide lacing or a good grade of belt lacing. Wet the heel strap and shape it as shown at left.

Cross straps may be braided of soft leather and sewed to the sole

Enlarged view showing how thread is sewn.

Ankle straps should be pliable.

Leave about 2 inches beyond the heel. Moisten and bend to shape.

This type of sandal should be made of leather no thicker than ⅛ inch.

Below are shown some modern methods of fastening straps.

Fastening straps with tubular rivets.

Fastening with copper rivets.

Fastening with split rivets.

Method of sewing with waxed thread to prevent wearing out.

TANNING

The tanning method described on the following pages has been tried and found to work very well. When no wood ashes are available for removing the hair, slaked lime may be used. This can be bought in 50-pound paper bags. Use one pound for every gallon of water and mix enough to cover the hides. Leave the hides in this solution until the hair is easily removed. It may take from a few days to ten days. Keep hides covered with the solution and stir every day. There will be no odor.

Be very careful about the amount of formic acid that is used in the tanning. Read and follow the directions carefully. Breaking the hide is a real job for anything larger than a coon skin. But for small hides such as squirrel, mink, muskrat, coon, woodchuck, and the like, it is not too difficult. The moon iron is ideal for breaking small hides. For rat and squirrel skins, a common table knife may be used.

Snake skins can also be tanned by this method. Snake skins are quite thin and become brittle when dry. They have a thin layer of fat on them which must be carefully scraped off before tanning.

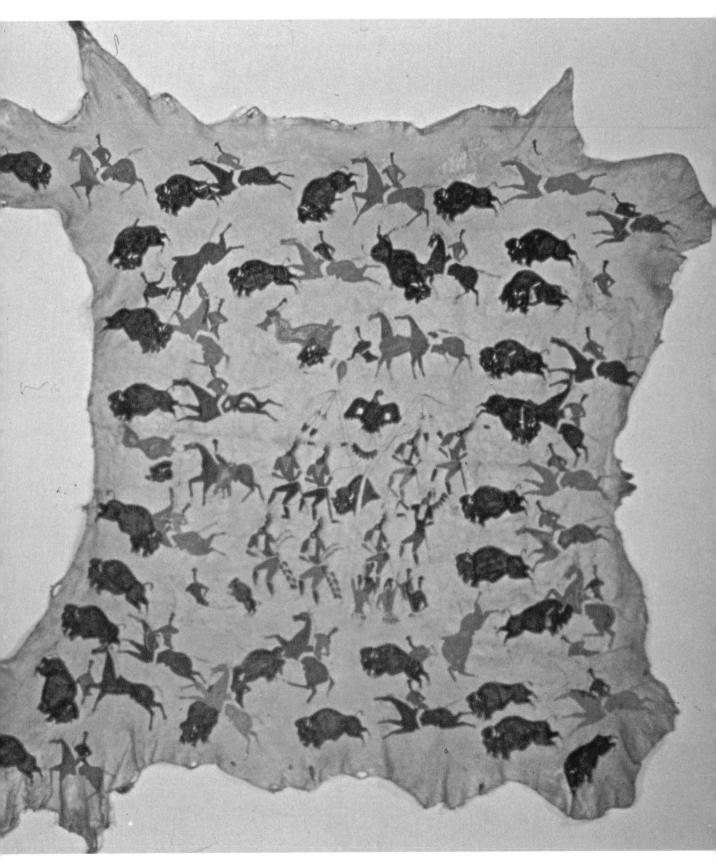

Painted elkskin of buffalo hunt; Shoshoni, Oklaho. Photograph courtesy
of Smithsonian Institution, National Museum of the American Indian.

A SIMPLE **TANNING** METHOD

The method described can be used at home or at a camp site, and if properly done, produces soft white skins. If you are not ready to tan immediately after skinning the animal, stretch the skin on a board or on the north side of some building. Scrape off every bit of flesh, fat and loose particles, rub salt into hide and let it dry. For tanning you will need formic acid (HCO_2H) which can be bought from a druggist, and sulphonated neetsfoot oil, which can be obtained from a tanner or a tanners' supply house. You'll also need water & coarse salt.

· FUR HIDES · · BUCKSKIN ·

Dried skins should be soaked in cold salt water over night, to soften them.

If hide is fresh, rub salt into it and hang it up overnight where it will keep moist. Then with fleshing tool and beam (Fig. 1 & 2) remove every bit of flesh, fat and loose underskin. Use a knife, but be very careful	*Take fresh hide as is, lay it fur side up and cover hair with clean wood ashes, sprinkle with water & roll up with hair inside. Leave in moist place a day or two. Unroll, wash thoroughly and remove hair and grain or scarfskin with fleshing knife. (Fig. 1 & 2) Also scrape flesh side clean*

······· *From here on all skins are handled in the same manner.*······

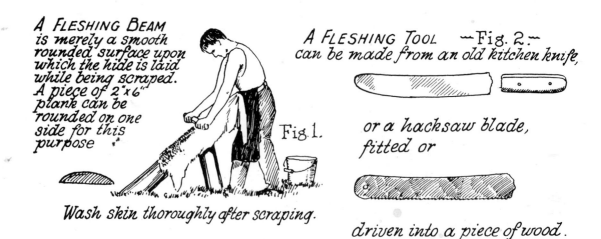

A FLESHING BEAM is merely a smooth rounded surface upon which the hide is laid while being scraped. A piece of 2"x 6" plank can be rounded on one side for this purpose

Fig. 1.

Wash skin thoroughly after scraping.

A FLESHING TOOL ~Fig. 2.~ can be made from an old kitchen knife,

or a hacksaw blade, fitted or

driven into a piece of wood.

NAIL →

It is sharpened like a cabinet scraper.

··· Soak all skins thoroughly before placing them into the solution.····

For skins up to size of 'coon or fox –

Place in solution of 1 gal. cold water
1½ lbs coarse salt
and 18 c.c. formic acid.
See that skin is covered and has no air pockets. Let it soak for 2 or 3 days, moving it around occasionally. Then take skin out of solution and add 2 c.c. of formic acid for skins the size of squirrel, and 3 c.c. for 'coon skin size. Do not add any for rabbit skins.

Use a stone jar for the solution and keep it covered while skins are being tanned. A five gallon jar is about the best size for small skins.

For calf or buckskins –
Place in solution of 1 gal. cold water
1½ lbs. coarse salt
and 20 c.c. formic acid.
Treat same as small skins. After 2 or 3 days add 1 to 5 c.c. of formic acid. depending on size and thickness of skin. Stir the additional acid into the original solution. Be sure to take skin out of solution while adding the additional acid.

If you have no C.C. (cubic centimeter) graduate, have the druggist put the smaller amount of acid into the bottle, paste a sticker to show the level, and then add the larger amount. When ready to use it, pour out the larger amount first.

TANNING (CONTINUED)

The skin is left in the solution for a week, but should be stirred around every day. In case you are busy with something else, skins can be left in the formic acid bath for as long as two or three weeks without harm. When skin is taken out, give it a quick rinse in cold water to remove most of salt. (Do not let it soak in rinse water.) Wring or squeeze as much of the moisture out of the skin as you can. Spread it out, flesh side up, and rub in a mixture of ½ sulphonated neetsfoot oil and ½ water. See that you rub it into every part of the skin. Rub in enough to thoroughly soak it or until it begins to look wet again, but not sloppy wet.

Now hang it up in a shady place until it shows signs of drying

BREAKING THE HIDE TO SOFTEN IT —

is the next operation and it should be done while the skin is still damp. If for some reason it should become dry, sprinkle it with ivory soap water, and roll it up for an hour or so until it becomes damp all over.

THE WHITE MAN'S SPADE SCRAPER

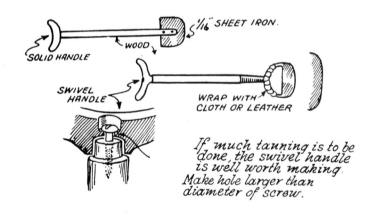

SOLID HANDLE
WOOD
5/16" SHEET IRON.

SWIVEL HANDLE
WRAP WITH CLOTH OR LEATHER

If much tanning is to be done, the swivel handle is well worth making. Make hole larger than diameter of screw.

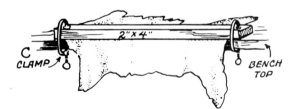

2"x4"

C CLAMP

BENCH TOP

Hide clamped to edge of work bench for breaking. The hide is shifted as work progresses. With this method, only the spade scraper can be used as shown below.

THE INDIAN'S RUBBING STICK

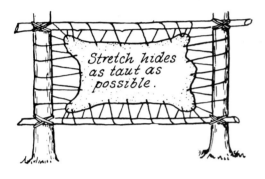

Make this of hard wood, if you have it, but soft wood will do.

Shape to chisel edge

Stretch hides as taut as possible.

The Indian method of stretching hide for breaking & softening.

Or the hide may be stretched on a movable frame of heavy poles. Then with the rubbing stick or the spade scraper, the hide is rubbed or scraped up & down, from left to right, in every direction & from both sides if it is to be buckskin. Only the flesh side is rubbed for fur tanning.

Breaking or softening a hide calls for a lot of elbow grease mixed with the sulphonated neetsfoot oil. It means working until the skin has become dry and soft. Keep the rubbing stick quite sharp. Press as hard as you dare while you are rubbing. Sometimes more neetsfoot oil and water must be applied if certain spots require it. But keep at it, rubbing & resting, & then rubbing some more. The softness of the skin depends upon how much you work it. Keep on rubbing until the skin is perfectly dry. If not, you will have a stiff hide and must start all over again with the neetsfoot oil and water.

Small skins such as squirrel or muskrat can be softened by rubbing and pulling or by pulling over a sharp edge such as a moon iron. Rabbit skins are simply rubbed between the hands as they are very thin.

Hold with one hand and rub with the other, up and down, side ways and cross ways.

Sheet iron →

Wood →

MOON IRON

P.S. Try a small skin first. W.B.H.

41

BUCKSKIN SHIRTS

The word *buckskin* is synonymous with the great American outdoors.

What is buckskin? Buckskin is tanned deerskin and nothing else. The Indians and the early settlers used the brain tanning method of preparing it. This method is not tanning in the strict sense of the word, but rather a preparation of the hide. It is done by rubbing or working the brain of the deer into the fresh or soaked hide until it is soft and pliable.

Smoke tanning is done by smoking a hide that has been brain tanned. The pitch from the smoke permeates the hide, preventing it from becoming stiff and hard after it has been wet. So an Indian smoke-tanned hide is one that has not only been brain tanned, but also smoked. It is well to keep in mind that an Indian always removes the scarfskin before tanning.

The usual commercial method of preparing buckskin is called chrome tanning. The scarfskin or grain is always left on unless otherwise stated. These skins are also very soft and pliable when finished.

Rawhide is just what the name implies: a raw hide stretched, fleshed, sometimes dehaired, and dried. Rawhide is hard and stiff when dry, while buckskin is soft and pliable.

There seems to be no limit to what can be done to make a buckskin shirt attractive. Wherever you see pictures of Indians, it is almost certain that some Indians are shown wearing buckskin shirts, and the ornamentation on every shirt is different. They are usually ornamented very elaborately and represent hours and sometimes months of work. Besides this, the Indians used an endless variety of material in decorating their shirts. There is no need to stick closely to any particular design. If the skins are larger or smaller, change the design so as not to waste material. If the fringe in some parts seems too short, an added piece of buckskin can be sewn into the seam to make the fringe longer. Indians designed their pictorial representation of historic events in what they called their "winter counts." These winter counts were drawn on whole skins and gave the story of the life of an Indian or of a whole tribe in pictorial form.

However, if designs and symbols are painted onto the skin with watercolor, the garments made of them cannot be readily washed or cleaned.

Made by village farmers of the plains. Photograph courtesy of Smithsonian Institution, National Museum of the American Indian.

Indian Buckskin Shirt-

The shirt described here was made from one large smoke tanned buckskin and was somewhat longer in front than the drawing shows. The shirt made by the author was from a smaller smoke tanned hide, and the bottom fringe added to give it a longer appearance. These hides were about 4 to 4½ ft. long by 2 ft. wide thru the center. Thin split cowhide (*glove leather*), sheepskin, suede, or any soft cream or buff colored leather may be used. Two smaller skins can also be used as shown in Fig.1, and sewed or laced together on the shoulders as shown in Fig.2. Outer edges of sleeves and bottom of shirt should be left rough. The shirt described is about a size 16.

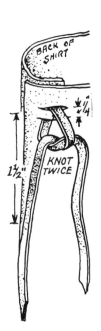

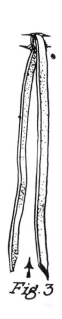

Fig. 3

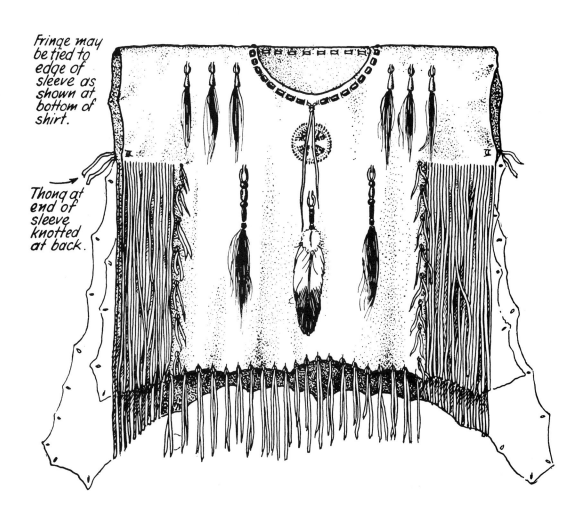

Fringe may be tied to edge of sleeve as shown at bottom of shirt.

Thong at end of sleeve knotted at back.

When shirt becomes soiled, untie all thongs, remove the ornaments, and spread shirt out on flat surface. Scrub lightly with hand brush moistened with soap suds. (Not too much) Wipe off with a clean cloth. When dry it can be softened again by rubbing the hide with your hands.

— SOMETIMES CALLED A SCALP SHIRT.

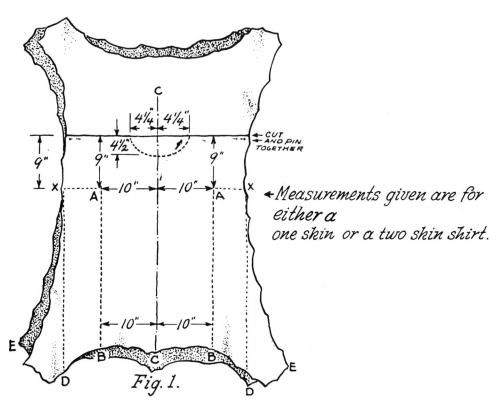

CUT AND PIN TOGETHER

Measurements given are for either a one skin or a two skin shirt.

Fig. 1.

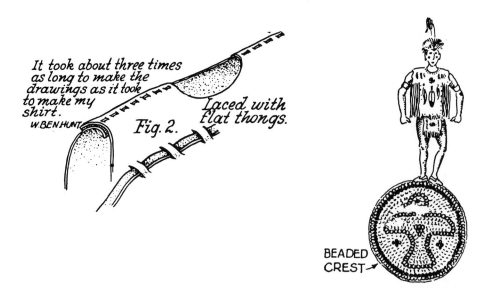

It took about three times as long to make the drawings as it took to make my shirt.
W. BEN. HUNT

Laced with flat thongs.

Fig. 2.

BEADED CREST

•1• If one skin is used, fold it as shown on large drawing. If two skins are used, cut skins to length wanted, and fasten upper edges together with pins.

•2• From center line CC, measure 4¼ inches each way, making a neck opening 8½ inches wide.

•3• Leave back of opening straight and cut front of neck opening in a half circle of about 4½ inches in diameter.

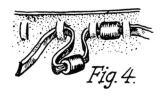

Fig. 4.

•4• On the two skin shirt, sew or lace upper seam. Fig. 2.

•5• Now measure 10 inches on either side of center line, (Do your marking with a pointed stick,) and mark as shown in Fig. 1, A B.

•6• Measure 9 inches down from shoulder seam on AB and mark to edge of skin, AX. Tie front and back together at X.

•7• Make straight cut from B to A on front and back.

•8• Now cut fringe ¼ inch wide until sections XED are cut off. (See Fig. 1, and drawing at left.)

•9• Cut thongs from cut off sections.

•10• Cut slots along sides AB, and tie as shown in Fig. 3.

•11• Cut slots at X, X, and tie.

•12• If necessary, tie fringe at bottom of shirt front.

•13• Cut slots around edge of neck opening and lace with thong and large beads, Fig. 4. Thong keeps opening from stretching.

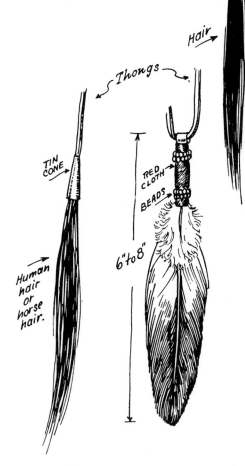

•14• Make ornaments as shown above and fasten with thongs as shown on large drawing.

•15• Crest may be beaded on a small piece of buckskin, trimmed flush, and sewed onto front of shirt. This is easier than beading directly onto the shirt.

SIOUX GHOST SHIRTS

Most of the Sioux who took part in the "battle" of Wounded Knee in December 1890 wore ghost shirts. Just before the battle, Yellow Bird, a medicine man, told the Indians that these shirts were "medicine" against the white man's bullets. This did not prove to be true, and the Indians—men, women, and children—were shot down. Sitting Bull, then a chief of the Sioux, became a leader in the ghost dances which became very popular among many of the Plains Indians.

The ghost shirts were made similar to the way described, but, of course, no two of the shirts were ever decorated alike. Some of these old muslin shirts look for all the world as though they had been made of buckskin. Some were said to have been smoked to give them a buckskin color. The muslin was first dipped in beige dye to give it the proper tint, then run through a clothes wringer about ten times, and then hung up to dry. While still slightly damp it was ironed. Since the small wrinkles caused by the wringing could not be ironed out, they gave the material the appearance of real buckskin.

If carefully done, the painted "beadwork" designs look very nice. One shirt seen at Hardin, Montana, had real beadwork sewed on the shirt, but most shirts were painted.

The best grade of unbleached muslin can be bought for very little. A fine ceremonial shirt, including large beads for the triangular flaps at the front and back of the neck opening, can thus be made for a small amount of money.

The simplest and easiest method of decorating cloth is with colored wax crayons. Thinned-down enamels can also be used. Because these clothes do not require frequent washing, water or poster color creates the nicest effect. These colors may be applied much more easily if a wetting agent or a little detergent is added to the paints.

Beaded buckskin dress; Plains. Photograph courtesy of Milwaukee Public Museum.

SIOUX GHOST SHIRT

The Indians made their Ghost Shirts of unbleached muslin and decorated them with paints as we are showing here.
3½ yards of 36" material is enough for sizes up to 16 or 17.

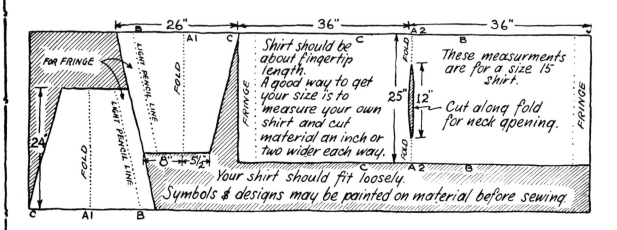

Shirt should be about fingertip length.
A good way to get your size is to measure your own shirt and cut material an inch or two wider each way.

These measurments are for a size 15 shirt.

Cut along fold for neck opening.

Your shirt should fit loosely.
Symbols & designs may be painted on material before sewing.

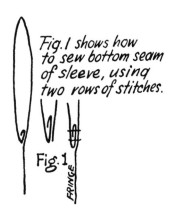

Fig. 1 shows how to sew bottom seam of sleeve, using two rows of stitches.

Fig. 1

Symbols & designs can be painted on cloth with water colors. When dry, go over painted part with a thin coat of clear lacquer or white shellac. Ghost shirts were always sewn with sinew, but a good thread to use is Barbours Linen thread No. 25. It should be waxed thoroughly. Sometimes the fringe was painted red. On some shirts a 4 or 5 inch strip of 12 or 14 inch fringe was added to the fringe of the sleeves at the elbow and half way down the side seam. (shown above) The bottom of the shirt was not always fringed.

To sew together, place A1 on A2 & pin the sleeve onto the shirt. Then sew the sleeve from C to B. After both of these seams are sewed, sew along the bottom of sleeves and then down the sides of shirt from armpit to X.

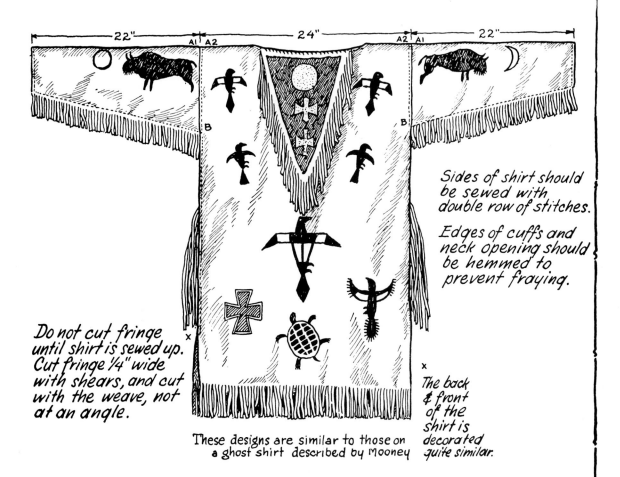

Sides of shirt should be sewed with double row of stitches.

Edges of cuffs and neck opening should be hemmed to prevent fraying.

Do not cut fringe until shirt is sewed up. Cut fringe ¼" wide with shears, and cut with the weave, not at an angle.

These designs are similar to those on a ghost shirt described by Mooney

The back & front of the shirt is decorated quite similar.

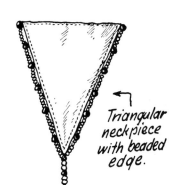

Triangular neckpiece with beaded edge.

INDIAN LEGGINGS
AND BREECHCLOUT

Up to about seventy-five years ago, the breechclout and moccasins were about all the "clothes" an Indian wore around camp, on hunting trips, and in battle. These "clothes" gave him the freedom he liked. In hunting he could feel every thorn or twig before it made any noise to disclose his approach. This would not have been the case had he worn more clothes. His life often depended on stealth, and stealth meant absolute quiet.

Leggings were used for dress occasions, as were shirts, vests, and the like. Today, of course, the Indian dresses much the same way we do, except for special occasions.

When wearing leggings, there is always a certain amount of "Indian" showing between the breechclout and the legging, but somehow it seems all right for an Indian to dress this way.

We often see the modern Indian wearing shorts, however, where brown skin should be. Some time ago, the author saw a very clever outfit worn by a Winnebago chief. It was a pair of washed-out khaki pants, very much the color of buckskin. On this, triangular flaps of the same color were sewed to give the appearance of leggings. These flaps were edged with red cloth and a 3-inch strip of beadwork was sewed to the pant cuffs. For a breechclout, a piece of black velveteen about 12–14 inches wide and 18–20 inches long was sewed to the top edge of the pants in front and back. The left half of the front piece was probably sewed directly to the pants, and the right half was buttoned over at the upper right corner. These two parts of the breechclout were richly beaded and edged with red cloth.

While this costume was not strictly according to Indian traditions, this Indian was very attractive in his beaded vest, bright-colored shirt, and headdress.

Group of men in costume on horseback; Blackfoot, Montana. Photo by Fred R. Meyer, courtesy of Smithsonian Institution, National Museum of the American Indian.

INDIAN LEGGINGS AND BREECHCLOUT

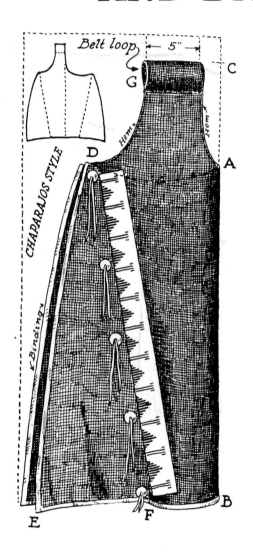

CHAPARAJOS STYLE

Belt loop

G

5"

C

Hem

Hem

D

A

E

F

B

Measure before buying material
C – Upper belt line.
A – Crotch
B – Ankle
D – Hip.
From C to B plus 4 inches will
  give length of material for
  one legging.
Material is usually 36 inches
  wide.
Fold and mark with chalk
  from A to D at crotch,
  from B to F at ankle (loose fit)
  from A to C as shown, and
  from D to G as shown,
Make flaps D,E,F about
8 or 10 inches wide at
bottom (from F to E)

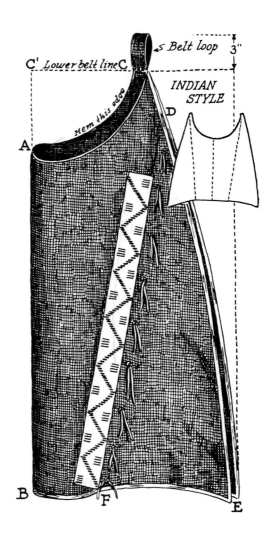

Belt loop 3"

C' Lower belt line C

INDIAN STYLE

Hem this edge

D

A

B

F

E

C - on this pattern is the lower belt line.

C to B is the length of material for one legging.

Measurements are same as at left except at A-C.

Measure from C' to bottom of crotch to determine where to start cutting at A.

Material for loop is taken from waste and is sewed on after legging proper is finished.

Before doing any sewing, it is good policy to pin them together and try them on, or do it with one and then cut the other one from that. Remember - one is left and one is right.

The Indian used whatever material was on hand. When game was plentiful, buckskin was used for all clothes. Later he used blanket cloth. Leggings may be made of buckskin if you have it or of split cowhide of a cream or gray color, such as is commonly called glove leather. Dark blue broadcloth is ideal but rather expensive. Outing flannel is often used but should be a good quality. A good grade of dark blue denim will make dandy leggings and is inexpensive. The cheapest material of all is two new grain bags without printing on them. Dye them a dark, navy blue color. Anyone can do it by following the directions on the dye package. Rip open the sewing before dyeing. Use silk ribbon, bias binding, or 1-inch or 1½-inch strips can be cut from bright red or yellow cloth. You probably can get someone to sew the binding on with a sewing machine. If you are using leather, the edges D-E should be fringed. Upper part of cloth leggings should be hemmed.

Fastening the two flaps from D to F may be done by sewing, by lacing with a buckskin thong, (holes in cloth are made with an awl)

by tying with thongs,→ or by fastening with Concha buttons These can easily be made of copper, brass, pewter or heavy tin by hammering the metal down into a depression in

—Knot.

a block of wood, and filing the edges to shape. Punch holes for tying.

Hem →

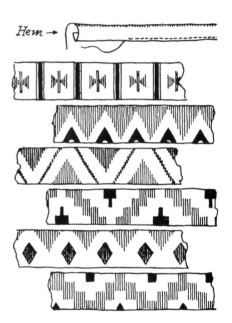

Suggested designs for beaded or painted legging strips. These strips are sewed to the leggings along all edges with overcast stitching.

Legging strips are usually beaded but they can also be made of strips of canvas carefully painted with bright colored enamel.

BREECHCLOUTS are

strips of soft cloth or buckskin
1 foot wide and 6 feet or more in
length. If made of cloth, the edges
are bound with red or yellow tape.
The ends are often beaded or sometimes the front end only is beaded.
The beads are sewn right onto the
cloth. Black cloth makes a wonderful
background for beadwork.
Note:- A breechclout may be worn without the leggings but it _must_ be worn
with them. Yes sir.

APACHE DESIGN

Fringe the ends
of a buckskin
breechclout.

How the breech-
clout is worn —
draped over the
front and back
of the belt.

THUNDERBIRD

INDIAN MOCCASINS

While the making of moccasins is quite simple, obtaining buckskin is rather a problem. Indian smoke-tanned buckskin is the best material for this project, but it is hard to get. However, if a regular tanned deerskin is obtainable, the scarfskin (the shiny side of the hide) may be removed very easily. To do this, cut out the moccasins, lay the piece of hide over the knee, and scrape off the scarfskin with the tooth side of a piece of hacksaw blade. Use a slant stroke for this work. After a few strokes of the saw blade, the scarfskin begins to roughen up and then disappear, leaving a nice, evenly roughened surface similar to the flesh side, but more evenly worked. Because moccasins are worn out of doors, they often get wet. When they dry, the leather often becomes hard and stiff. If rubbing them does not soften the leather, a little neats-foot oil will.

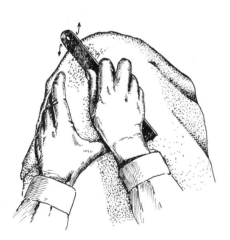

Fig. 1. Removing the scarfskin.

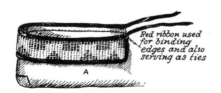

Red ribbon used for binding edges and also serving as ties

Fig. 2. Beading the flaps of the moccasin.

Beading the toe of the moccasin.

When beading on leather or buckskin, do not try to push the needle through the skin, but go just below the surface. For the side flaps the Indians sometimes do their beadwork on a loom and then sew it onto the leather. This also may be done on the toe of the moccasin, but it is best to sew the beadwork to a piece of cloth and then to the moccasin, being very careful to hide the edges of the cloth.

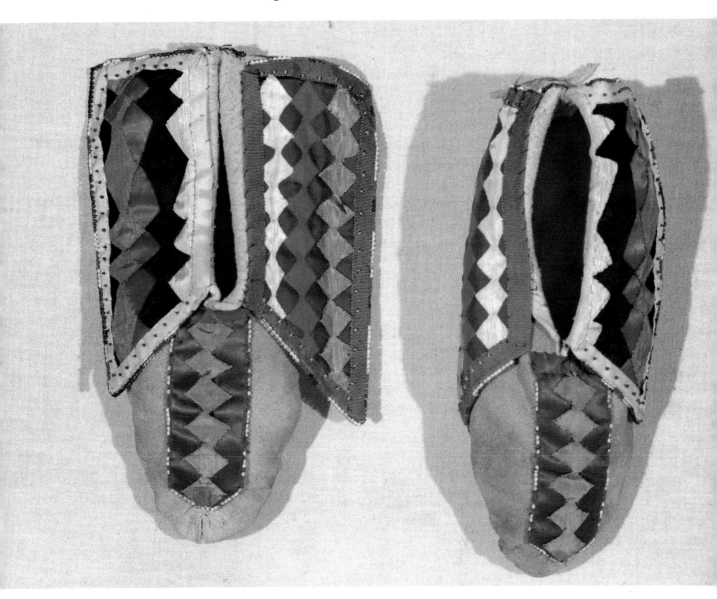

Ribbonwork moccasins; Fox. Photograph courtesy of Milwaukee Public Museum.

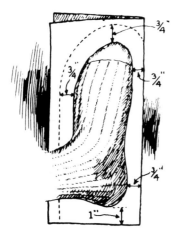

INDIAN MOCCASINS

1 Fold a piece of paper and place foot on it ¾" from fold. Draw a line ¾" away from toes to widest part of foot and then parallel with fold to about 1" beyond heel.
Cut out along dotted line.

4 Cut the leather around the outside only. Fold the outer side in and sew, starting at C and continuing to end.

— SEWING —

With a sharp awl punch about 7 or 8 holes 1⁄16" from the edge and 1⁄8" apart. Wax a piece of shoemakers linen thread and with a small darning needle sew up the part that is perforated as shown here. Pull each stitch as tightly as possible. Then punch another set of holes and sew. Do not try to punch all the way around at one time as the leather may pull out of shape. Don't punch holes too far from edge. Keep thread well waxed.

— TO MAKE AN AWL —

drive a nail into a ¾" dowel and file to a long point.

PATTERN —
for left foot use other side for right foot.

Cut pattern along the line A & B

4½"

2½"

2 Spread out the pattern. Then draw line A midway between edge and fold. Next draw line B at right angles to line A at point where foot is widest. Make length of line B equal to width of foot minus about 1". Dimensions shown above are for a size 8 foot.

3 Mark patterns on leather to be used. Soft tanned buckskin is best but any soft leather will do. Be sure to turn pattern over for the right foot. The one shown is the left one.

5 Turn moccasin right side out and cut lines A & B.

6 Cut two pieces of leather 2½" x 3" to be used as tongues

7 Sew tongues in place, using same stitch as before, and with the seam on the inside

8 Now slip the moccasin over the proper foot and determine the length as shown below. Mark with pencil and cut away surplus as shown below, E. Then cut in as shown at X, below, E and F

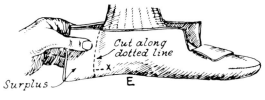

Cut along dotted line

Surplus

E

D

¾"
X   ¾"
F   ⌐1½"⌐   G
center fold

9 Turn moccasin inside out again and sew as shown at G - Try it on occasionly to be sure of a good fit.

10 The small flap G (right) may be cut off and the heel sewed straight across, H, while the moccasin is still turned inside out.

H

Or- the flap may be sewed up, I, in which case it should be sewed on the outside. Be sure that all stitches are pulled up tight and that the thread is well waxed.

11 Cut slots as shown below for the lacing. Cut the lacing from the same leather that was used for the moccasins.

12 The moccasins are now finished but a simple design of colored beads will add a great deal to their appearance

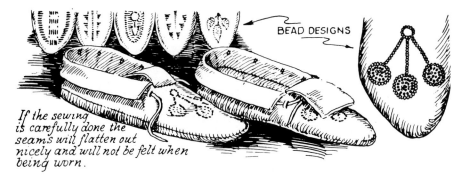

BEAD DESIGNS

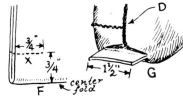

If the sewing is carefully done the seams will flatten out nicely and will not be felt when being worn.

CONCHA BELTS

For dress occasions the all-leather belts are no doubt the proper thing to wear, but for holding up a pair of jeans, a studded belt is right. Probably the finest of these ornamental belts are the Navajo concha belts. These are worn by nearly every Southwest Indian who can afford to own or make one. And, if he is not wearing it, he most likely has one put away somewhere for special occasions. The concha buttons used on these belts are almost always made of coin silver.

Coin silver, however, besides being rather expensive for the beginner, is also quite difficult to work and solder. Substitutes can be made, and of these, nickel silver is probably the best. Aluminum also may be used, and if necessary tin, which while being the least expensive material, may be so carefully made that tin concha belts will look quite good.

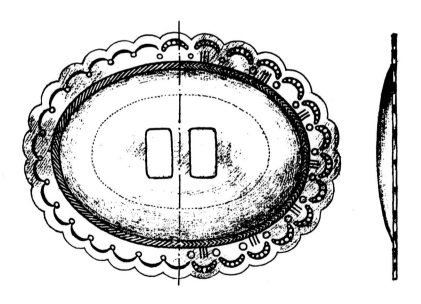

Concha

Pottery, by master potter Nampeyo; Tewa. Photograph courtesy of
Milwaukee Public Museum.

The two principal requirements for belt making are, of course, leather and buckles. Strap leather can be obtained, cut to size at harness shops or saddlery supply houses, or if a number of them are to be made, it will pay to get a half or a whole steer hide. The usual colors are black, brown & buff or natural.

MAKE A
BELT

Buckles come in all sizes and shapes. They can be taken from old discarded belts, or new ones can be bought at supply houses. They are usually made of brass and are often nickle plated. There are single and double buckles. Centerbar buckles do not require a loop for the end of the belt

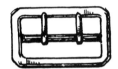
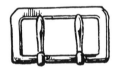

Centerbar buckle
2 inch double

Regular
tongue buckles

Centerbar
1¾ & 1½ inch single

Regular
tongue buckles

1 Mark & punch 2 holes and cut out between

Moisten leather and bend 2

3 Cut or punch holes & lace with thong or regular lacing.

Skive end about ¼ inch
Fastening centerbar buckle

64

4 To make loop for regular buckle :—
Measure off on _inner side_ of ½" strip
A — width of belt
B — 2½ times thickness of belt leather
C — ½ of width of belt.
  Also cut a piece of wood to
  these same dimensions.

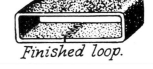

Finished loop.

5 Punch 4 holes about $\frac{3}{32}$ inches from
each end and lace together loosely with
waxed cord. Then pull up, bringing
ends together and knot. Moisten
leather and slip
it over the piece of
wood mentioned
in 4 & let it dry.

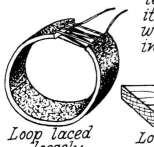

Loop laced
loosely.

Loop drying on stick.

6 The loop is then simply placed an inch or so back from the buckle
as shown at left, and laced or sewed. The loop
is left loose

7 When the buckle is fastened
neatly put the belt on and
mark where the hole (or holes) should
be and punch them. Then punch
one hole about an inch back to allow for stretching, and set
one the same distance ahead to allow for expansion caused
by mulligan stew, hamburgers, etc.

DECORATE THEM

This may be done with leather lacing, with brass or nickle-plated
spots, silver concha buttons, or a combination of both lacing and
metal. Lacing can be obtained at supply houses in different
widths, or it can be cut out of thin calf or goat skin

Note : If the leather is dry, it is good policy to give it a dressing of neats foot oil
   or saddle soap   Never try to work with dried-out leather.

8 Out of large nails make punches like those shown above   The single punches may be ³⁄₃₂ inch to ⅛ inch wide and the three-prong punch should be ³⁄₃₂ inch punches and ³⁄₃₂ inch spaces

9 Below are shown several methods of decorating with leather lacing or with colored artificial leather lacing which is sold under different names, such as protex, craftstrip, etc.

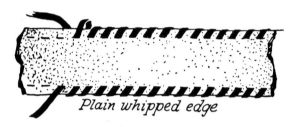

Plain whipped edge

Cross stitch

Staggered whipped edge

Holes made with round punch

Wide hand-cut lacing

10 Metal ornaments like those used to decorate harnesses, are called spots or studs and can be bought at harness supply houses in sizes ranging from ⅛ to 1 inch, and in various shapes. If spots are dull they should be given a good polishing before applying them.

Round

Oval

Peanut

Square

Star

Jeweled

66

11 Round and oval ornaments can also be made of copper, brass, aluminum, or monel metal. Hammer round or oval depressions into the end of a hardwood block Fig.1 Different shapes and sizes can be made with larger or smaller ball-peen hammers or with pieces of bar steel filed to shape.(Fig. 2.) Lay a piece of sheet metal over the depression & pound it down into it with the same tool used to make that particular depression. Prongs can be cut out with a small tin snips and then filed. Or ornaments can be finished like concha buttons, and sewed onto the belt.

Fig. 1

Bar steel filed round
Fig. 2

Concha button

12

A combination of leather lacing and studs

A few suggestive arrangements are shown below

Lay out ornaments to determine position on belt. Mark carefully where prongs come & punch holes with a chisel edged punch. (Shown in upper right hand corner)

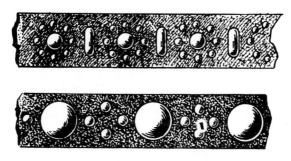

Then push the prongs through and bend them underneath. Hammer them down carefully, placing the spot on something soft to prevent denting.

CONCHAS

Concha is a Spanish word meaning shell or like a shell. Concha buttons, as we know them, are usually made of silver, more or less convex and ornamental. They are made by Mexican, Navajo and Zuni silversmiths to decorate belts, hat bands, chaps, etc. Navajo and Pueblo Indians use them to fasten their moccasins. Silver is expensive as well as hard to work, but we can use 18 gauge nickle silver or aluminum, or heavy tin for our purpose, and do a nice job, too. Nickle silver & tin can be soldered with 50-50 solder.

A few simple stamping tools are required. Two straight ones for lines can be made from small cold chisels,(— -) and should have rounded ends. For round tools use hollow point nail sets ○ ○ ○ • Then shapes like these ⌒ ⌒ can be made of ¼ inch drill rod, heated & hammered, then filed to shape and tempered.

Edges on these are filed flat.

And here are a few concha button designs to work from.

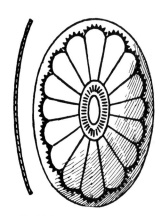

Solid concha with loops on concave side.

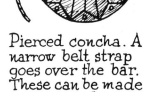

Pierced concha. A narrow belt strap goes over the bar. These can be made when using aluminum.

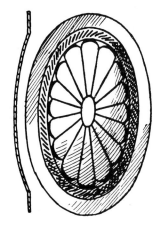

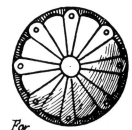

For hatbands or ornamental buttons.

Strap

Conchas may be from 1 to 3½ inches in length or in diameter.

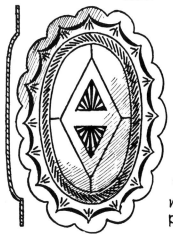

The inner triangles may be cut out if pierced button is desired.

① Lay out your design on a piece of tracing paper

② Make a template of the outline.

③ Scratch outline on metal, cut out the blanks with a tin shears and finish edges with a file.

④ Place carbon and tracing papers on disk and transfer design.

⑤ Now place the disk on a smooth piece of iron, (hardwood, if tin is used) and with a hammer and dies, incise the lines. Do not go too deep. This is not an embossing job. The idea is to make a nice well-defined depression. In making tin and aluminum conchas only light blows are struck, but with nickle silver it is different.

5 continued *Hold the die as shown, with the thumb and first two fingers, and hold down the disk with the third and fourth fingers.* *The third finger also acts as a guide for the tool. This requires a little practice and should be tried out on a piece of scrap metal first. Long lines are made by hitting lightly as the tool is moved along, and then going over again using harder blows. Use a hammer with a flat face. Other stampings are made with one blow*

6 *Now with a ball peen hammer form a shallow circular depression in a block of hard wood. End grain is preferable.*

Heel of hand rests on iron plate or bench.

IRON PLATE

Loops

7 *Place disc face down over the depression and carefully "bump it up", to form a shallow dome*

8 *Form loops out of 16 gauge copper or brass wire   to fit leather belt.   Leather belt is usually from ½ to ¾ inches wide.*

9 *Solder loops to back of concha; two for belts & hat bands, one in center of round buttons or ornamental conchas.*

A buckle can be made to match the conchas; the belt may be fastened with a small inconspicuous buckle, or with leather thongs.

BUCKLE

Six large conchas are enough for an ordinary belt. For a hat band, use 1 inch conchas and space them ½ inch apart

·Concha·Neckerchief·Slides·

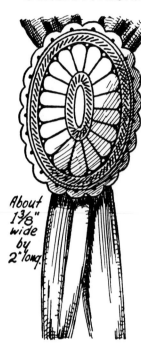

About 1⅜" wide by 2"long.

Make an extra fine concha for a neckerchief slide. The loops should be larger than for belt conchas & should be made of ¼" strips of the same material that is used for the concha. ∼

Concha·Watch·Fobs·

can be made by sewing strap to wire loops or by soldering one wire loop to the top

Notice how the cow's head is made with a few die punches.

MATERIALS AND DESIGNS

Before the white man came to this country, the Indians dressed in furs and buckskins that were decorated with quills, beads, and paint. Large beads, wampum, dyed porcupine, and feather quills were used for these decorations. When the white man brought small beads, the Indian quickly adopted them and used them instead of the more clumsy beads which had been made by the Indians themselves. They found these small beads were easier to work with, and they were available in many bright colors. The Plains Indians used paint to decorate their buffalo-hide tepees and their buckskin clothing. Paint was also used on winter counts or calendars. The Indian reckoned years by winters, and his counts or calendars took the form of pictorial records of the important events of each year.

The Indian used whatever material was handy. He took advantage of the white man's paints, beads, materials, dyes, and tools very quickly, but he stuck to his own designs and symbols. These are his heritage, handed down through generations of artists.

The plates of designs and decorations shown here have been especially included for those interested in Indian lore who cannot get to libraries and museums. Some of these designs are typical of certain tribes, but this need not create a problem. The Indians themselves use styles and designs of other tribes. But do not mix the designs of different tribes too much! A Sioux outfit

Belt; Chippewa. Photograph courtesy of Milwaukee Public Museum.

with a Navajo design is no more proper than a Zuñi mask would be at an Iroquois mask dance. Most of the designs for clothing shown in this book have been copied from the Plains Indians. In some cases the origin of the designs is hard to trace. While the Blackfoot Indians usually use geometric designs, there are many who also use floral designs which may have been borrowed from the Crows.

You may want to start a scrapbook of pictures showing authentic Indian apparel and equipment. The material shown in the plates on design was taken from the Smithsonian Institution's Bureau of American Ethnology books, the Milwaukee Public Museum, United States National Museum Reports, and other sources. Collecting the designs took hours of research. It is hoped they will help others in their Indiancraft hobby.

I·N·D·I·A·N · D·E·S·I·G·N·S

◄◄◄ *BUCKSKIN SHIRTS* ►►►

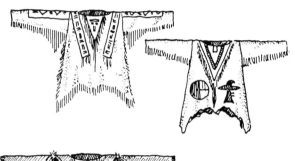

Here are shown four different types of war shirts and the ways in which they may be decorated. Be original but stick to the Indian designs.

►◄ *BEAD OR PAINT DESIGNS FOR SHIRTS* ►◄

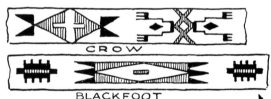
CROW

BLACKFOOT   ↳SHOULDER

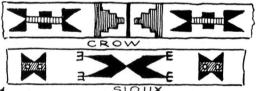
CROW

SIOUX

& ARM STRIPS ↗

FOR GHOST SHIRTS

◆ DESIGNS FOR VESTS ◆

SIOUX

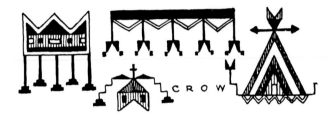

CROW

◄◄ LEGGING STRIPS ►►

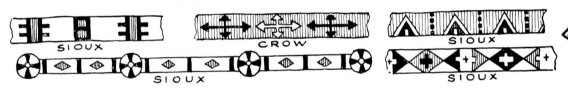

SIOUX   CROW   SIOUX

SIOUX   SIOUX

◄ BREECH CLOUT DESIGNS ►

CHEYENNE   SAUK   WINNEBAGO   CROW   SIOUX

A·N·D··D·E·C·O·R·A·T·I·O·N·S
▼·△·▼ WOODLAND BAG PATTERNS ▼·△·▼

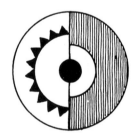

— SHIELD DESIGNS —

••• DESIGNS FOR TOM-TOMS •••

 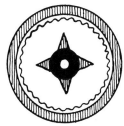  

NECK PIECE DESIGNS FOR SHIRTS

BLACK-FOOT

SIOUX

COILED BASKET AND PLAQUE DESIGNS

POMO   TULARE   NAVAHO   HAT CREEK   HOPI.

KERN

INDIAN SYMBOLS AND DESIGNS

Many books have been written about Indian symbols and designs. As many symbols as possible are shown in the plates in this chapter with the hope that they may be useful in the absence of a more comprehensive book of symbols.

Indians used any colors they could get, but reds, blues, yellows, and blacks were the most common. The reds varied from the brownish to bright vermilion, although crimson was not used.

The mediums for these symbols vary, depending on where they are used. Beadwork, of course, is in a class by itself. On leather, or canvas, paint is used. It may be house paint, enamel, or lacquer, but it should not be put on too thickly. Water color is often used on bows, handles or rattles, Hopi dolls, and similar projects. If the objects are to be frequently handled, a coat of shellac or varnish will keep the water colors from smudging. In making peace pipes out of wood or clay, the outline of the symbols can be incised, or scratched into the material. The oil paints used should be the flat wall-paint type. Use this for the base coat and mix tube paints with it for the colors.

Beaded apron; Chippewa. Photograph courtesy of Milwaukee
Public Museum.

INDIAN SYMBOLS & DESIGNS

HORSE

DEER

HORSE
(*Journey*)

DOG

DEER

DEER TRACKS
(*Plenty game*)

WARRIOR ON HORSE

BUFFALO

REPEAT FOR BORDER

COYOTE TRACK BORDER

TRACKS

(*Bright prospects*)

THUNDERBIRDS
(*Sacred bearer of happiness*)

BEAR TRACKS
(*Good omen*)

SQUAW

MEN
(*Human life*)

BORDER DESIGN

BUTTERFLIES
(*Everlasting life*)

RAIN CLOUDS
(Good prospects)

SUN
(Happiness)

TRACKS

BIRDS

EAGLE
FEATHERS
(Chief)

OWL

(Signs
of the
desert)

CACTUS

GILA MONSTER

BIRD

CLOUDS

LIGHTNING

RAIN
DROP
(Good crops)

RAIN

SUN RAYS
(Constancy)

CREE DESIGN

RATTLE-
SNAKE JAW
(Strength)

MOUNTAINS

CHEYENNE
CRESTS

BLACKFEET
MOTIFS

CHIPPEWA
MOCCASIN ORNAMENT

MEXICAN INDIAN DESIGN

WINNEBAGO BANDS

HUPA BASKET DESIGNS

BLANKET ORNAMENT

BAND DESIGN

BAND DESIGN

WATER SNAKE

The Indian symbols and designs shown here were collected from many sources. They will be found valuable in ornamenting such articles as moccasins, headbands, vests, knife sheaths, tepees, war drums, tom-toms and the like.

INDIAN BEADWORK

Indian beadwork must be seen to be appreciated. The love of pretty things and the patience possessed by the American Indian, make him a master at designing and executing beadwork. Indian bead designs are not simply meaningless areas of color, but in nearly every case, possess deep symbolic meaning.

Before attempting to bead a vest or headdress, or any of the many things that are beaded, try to visit a museum and study some of the beadwork made by the Indians. The plate on page 84 shows how the beads are fastened to the fabric. Nothing will make an Indiancraft enthusiast quite so proud as to be able to answer "I made it" when asked, "Where did you get that fine piece of beadwork?"

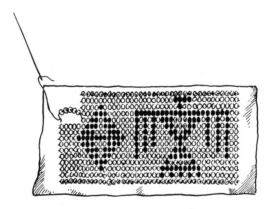

John Moosehart in costume; Menominee, Wisconsin. Photograph
courtesy of Milwaukee Public Museum.

INDIAN BEADWORK

While the Indians used any and every kind of beads obtainable the prettiest work was made with opaque glass beads. However, transparent beads look equally pretty on certain materials.

WARP THREADS

NAIL

NAIL

ABOUT 4" LONGER THAN THE WORK TO BE PRODUCED

End pieces may be fastened from below with two screws each so they may be changed when shorter work is done. This simple loom is used for belts, headdress bands or any other narrow beaded strips

Cuts

End piece of loom. Make cuts with fine coping saw about 1/16 apart and 1/16 deep.

2½

2½   ⅞"

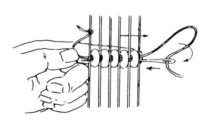

① *String required number of beads on thread, hold them in place on underside of warp and bring thread over end warp thread and back thru above the warp.*

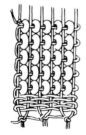

② *Finish by weaving back and forth and then knotting ends.*

Always use uneven number of beads across. Use waxed buttonhole twist for warp and also for threading beads. Special beading needles should be used for glass beads. For wooden beads use an ordinary thin sewing needle.

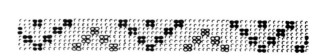

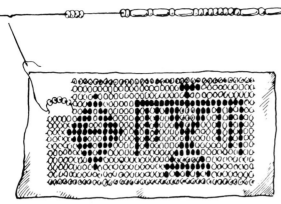

A method of applying beads to cloth or buckskin. Usually five beads are threaded and sewed in place at each operation. Care should be taken to keep the rows even. This type of work is used on buckskin vests, shirts, leggings, etc.

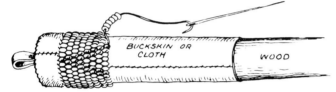

BUCKSKIN OR CLOTH   WOOD

Beaded handles on drum sticks, rattles, etc. are made by first covering the stick with soft leather or cloth and then sewing the beads on with waxed thread in groups of 4 or 5, running spirally. Notice that beads are staggered. Cover end of stick with leather.

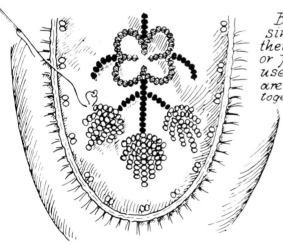

Beads on moccasins are sewed on singly because of the hard wear they recieve. Frequently only a leaf or flower design like the above is used without a background (Beads are sewed on before moccasins are sewed together.)

VESTS

Let's start with the buckskin vest. This type of vest is usually made of oil or chrome-tanned buckskin. A vest lining is used only when working with very thin skins. Some buckskin is almost too thick for vests; to make a nice vest, it should be of medium thickness. Some vests are fringed at the bottom and some down the side seams. Concha buttons can be used on the pockets and back, and small patches of beadwork help to decorate the vests.

Vests of unborn calfskin are always popular. They are the easiest to make, but the skins are scarce. The one shown was made of black and white skin and was bound with thin black horsehide sewn on by machine.

Full beaded vests are highly prized by the Indians. Their price can be $50 to $200 and more, depending on the design and workmanship. One vest that was sewed with sinew and had every second bead fastened was priced at $225. The beads were carefully selected and were very uniform in size. Although few people like these vests enough to make one, we have drawn one with a Plains Indian design which could be used as a pattern. The designs could also be painted on.

Men in costume; Chippewa. Photograph courtesy of Milwaukee
Public Museum.

BEADED INDIAN VESTS

Beaded vests are usually made of smoke tanned buckskin, but that is rather hard to get. A full beaded vest can be made of any soft leather because, unless left unlined, no leather shows. For a partly beaded vest, any soft leather that has had the grain or scarf skin removed may be used. It should be natural or buckskin color. The beads are sewed directly onto the leather in strings of from two to six or eight beads as shown below. Draw outline of figures onto leather with a pencil.

Red flannel binding.

COLORS OF BEADS
Eagles - *blue & white.*
One horse - *dark blue & white. One, orange.*
One Indian, *red, the other, yellow.*
War bonnets *of white & black beads.*
Lower band, *dark blue edges, red & yellow tepees*
Buffalo, *of very dark blue beads.*

A PARTLY BEADED VEST

This type of vest is very attractive and is not very difficult to make. The Sioux vest shown is very similar to the one given to the author by Chief Lone Eagle. Two methods of sewed bead work are shown in the two vests on this page. The beads on both vests are sewed directly to the buckskin, but as you will notice, they are sewed in almost any direction in the animal and bird designs, while in the geometric designs they are all laid in one direction, except at the neck and arms of the one shown below. While most Indians fasten the sinew as shown below, some, like the Crows sewed through the leather. Modern Crow beadwork is sewed with thread. When sewing with thread do not put more than eight beads to a stretch. Using sinew, as many as ten to fifteen beads are strung between fastenings.

Draw guide lines with a pencil to insure even work. You may have to add a bead to a string now and then to even up the line.

For ceremonial purposes, vests can be made of suede or split cowhide and the designs carefully painted on with bright colored enamels. Sometimes you will have to give it a second coat, if the leather is very porous.

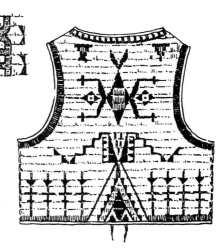

A FULL BEADED VEST

Here is something you can really sink your teeth into. It's a real job for anyone and worth the effort. Note how the sides are cut. White or turquois beads make a dandy background.

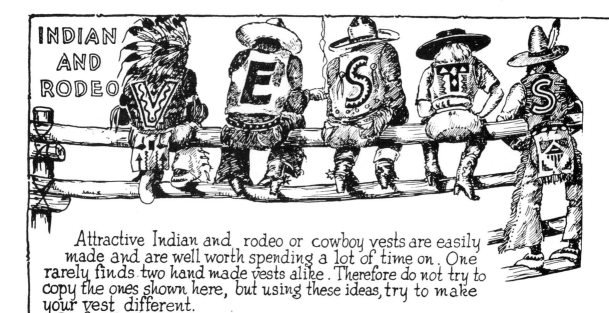

INDIAN AND RODEO

Attractive Indian and rodeo or cowboy vests are easily made and are well worth spending a lot of time on. One rarely finds two hand made vests alike. Therefore do not try to copy the ones shown here, but using these ideas, try to make your vest different.

By far the best and safest way to get your pattern is to take it from your own vest or one that fits you. It need not be ripped apart. Lay it on a piece of heavy wrapping paper, trace around and allow about ¼ inch wherever there are seams. Then lay the pattern on the material, mark and cut it. These vests should fit rather loosely.

BUCKSKIN VESTS ···

Most vests can be made of 3 pieces — the two front pieces and the back.

← *Two piece pocket*

Fringed trimming

If thin buckskin is used, it is advisable to line it with cloth, as buckskin sometimes has a way of pulling out of shape. Split cowhide, calfskin, and suede leather does not stretch so readily. Edges may be finished or bound in several ways →

CALF SKIN VESTS···

These are usually made of unborn calf skins. Spotted black and white or brown and white, make the nicest vests. The edges are bound with some thin leather such as suede leather, sheepskin or thin calf or horsehide.

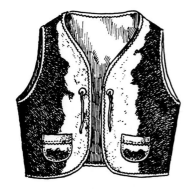

Binding leather can be cut with a pinking shears.
A red lining was used in this vest to add color to it.
Vests made of calf or buckskin can be sewed by machine without trouble.

The back of this vest was made from the center of the hide and the front was matched as evenly as possible from pieces cut from the edges or belly section. The edges are bound with thin horsehide.

ROACH

Headdresses and war bonnets were worn according to the Indian's locality. An Indian with a long-tailed eagle-feather headdress would not get along very well in thickly wooded districts. It was probably in these wooded sections that the roach originated. The best roaches were made from the guard hair of the porcupine; and since each porcupine produced few of these hairs (a bundle about ½ to ⅝ inch in diameter), it would take many porcupines to make a roach. For this reason, it is suggested that fiber be used for making roaches. The use of fiber also has another advantage, because the doubling up of the fiber leaves no short ends to take care of. Before bending the fiber over the cord, be sure to arrange it unevenly as shown in Figure 2 on page 95, or you will have a sort of cropped effect when finished. Sometimes a narrow strip of fur is sewn around the edge of the base for variety. Rabbit, muskrat, or mink fur will be found suitable for this.

Buffalo headdress; Plains. Photograph courtesy of Milwaukee Public Museum.

Louis Corbine in costume at Milwaukee Midsummer Festival, 1936; Chippewa. Photograph courtesy of Milwaukee Public Museum.

Louis White in costume at Milwaukee Midsummer Festival, 1936; Chippewa. Photograph courtesy of Milwaukee Public Museum.

We cannot all be chiefs, but we can be good warriors, and as such should be "well dressed". A roach is an attractive head ornament for any warrior and is not hard to make

A CHEYENNE ROACH

Roaches were and are still worn by both Plains and Woodland Indians. Some are made by simply cutting a strip of deerskin with the hair on it, from the rump part of the hide.

This is dyed red and worn as shown. Some were made of horsehair, some of porcupine guard hair and some of a combination of both. The roach from which the one described here was copied, was made of porcupine guard hair.

Some Indians shaved their heads leaving a scalp lock of long hair. The roach was tied to this scalp lock, but nowadays a harness is made to fit the head and the roach is fastened permanently to the harness. The sketch shows this method. If horsehair is not available, use manila or sisal fiber. This can be bought in bundles or can be obtained by untwisting binder twine and soaking it until it becomes straight. Dry it and sort out the best fiber.

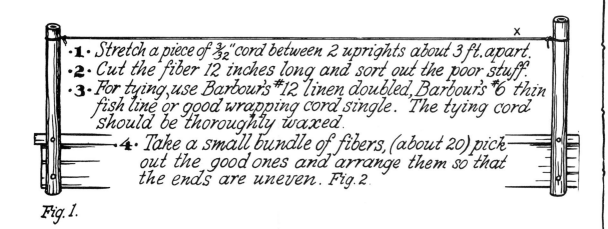

·1· Stretch a piece of ³⁄₃₂" cord between 2 uprights about 3 ft. apart.
·2· Cut the fiber 12 inches long and sort out the poor stuff.
·3· For tying, use Barbour's #12 linen doubled, Barbour's #6 thin fish line or good wrapping cord single. The tying cord should be thoroughly waxed.
·4· Take a small bundle of fibers, (about 20) pick out the good ones and arrange them so that the ends are uneven. Fig. 2.

Fig. 1.

Fig. 2.

·5· Knot one end of waxed tying cord to main cord. (X Fig. 1.)
·6· Bend the bundle of fiber in the middle, over the cord and tie as shown in drawings below.

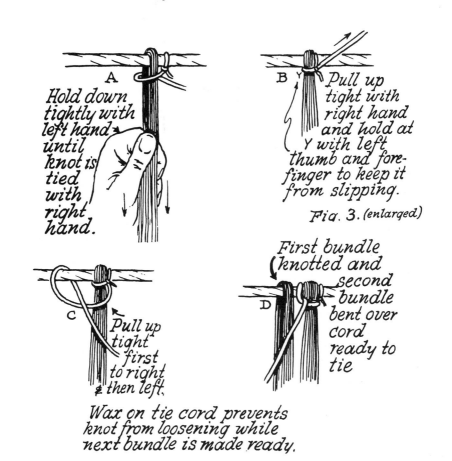

A — Hold down tightly with left hand until knot is tied with right hand.

B — Pull up tight with right hand and hold at Y with left thumb and forefinger to keep it from slipping.

Fig. 3. (enlarged)

C — Pull up tight first to right & then left.

D — First bundle knotted and second bundle bent over cord ready to tie

Wax on tie cord prevents knot from loosening while next bundle is made ready.

A CHEYENNE ROACH

·7· *Ten bunches of fiber to the inch on the main cord are the proper number to use. When finished these look like Fig. 4*

Side toward you

Fig. 4
(enlarged)

Tie bunches of fiber as tight & close as possible.

Opposite side. This will be toward outside on roach.

8· *Now tie for 14 inches in this manner & knot tie cord onto main cord. Cut off main cord one in. beyond fiber at both ends.*

·9· *For coloring use permanent black, brown, and red ink, (the author uses black and brown shoe dye). With a brush or a dauber, color the fiber as shown at left using short strokes toward the ends of fiber. Colors should sort of blend into each other in an uneven line. Color both sides. It's a good idea to try coloring a single bundle of fiber first.*

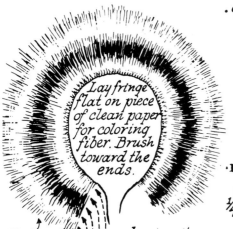

Lay fringe flat on piece of clean paper for coloring fiber. Brush toward the ends.

Ends red
1" of brown
1½" of black
1" of brown
White or natural

Laying it this way spreads the fibers better.

·10·

⅛ inch apart

Fig. 6

Holes

BASE

6"

¼

1½

1½"

Cut base of 1⁄16" or 3⁄32" leather and punch holes with an awl. Fig. 6. Or use 2 thicknesses of felt.

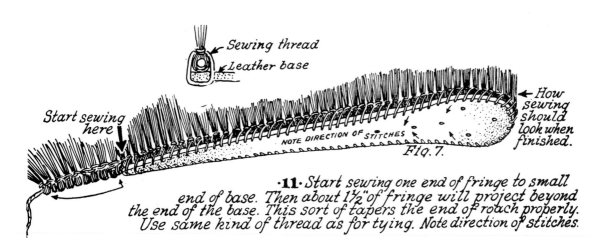

Sewing thread

Leather base

Start sewing here

How sewing should look when finished.

NOTE DIRECTION OF STITCHES

Fig. 7.

·11· *Start sewing one end of fringe to small end of base. Then about 1½" of fringe will project beyond the end of the base. This sort of tapers the end of roach properly. Use same kind of thread as for tying. Note direction of stitches.*

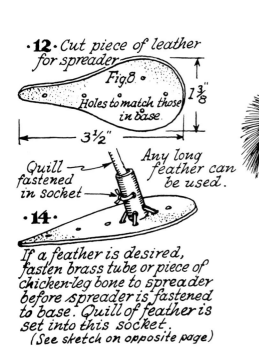

Fig. 9.

·12· *Cut piece of leather for spreader.*

Fig. 8.

Holes to match those in base.

$1\frac{3}{8}$

$3\frac{1}{2}$"

Quill fastened in socket

Any long feather can be used.

·14·

If a feather is desired, fasten brass tube or piece of chicken-leg bone to spreader before spreader is fastened to base. Quill of feather is set into this socket.

(See sketch on opposite page)

Fig. 10.

·13· *When spreader is tied to the upper side of base, inside the fringe, it will force the fiber outward at that part. Tie it down firmly to base. Fig. 9.*

Band may be beaded

·15· *A head harness like this may be made to fasten roach to, or the roach can be sewed onto a skull cap made from the top of a ladie's tan stocking which gives the head a shaved appearance. Fig. 10.*

WAR BONNETS AND HEADDRESSES

A young boy once asked where he could get eagle feathers. This question is not foolish at all! It is quite the natural thing for someone who is interested in Indian lore to want a war bonnet of eagle feathers. The dark-tipped eagle feather is symbolic of the American Indian, and is desired by any true Indian enthusiast.

Through the efforts of the Audubon Society, it is unlawful to shoot golden eagles or to sell their feathers. But you can buy imitation eagle feathers. These are white feathers with the tip dyed a dark brown, and they look very realistic. You will need about 30 feathers. Then you need fluffs, horsehair, and the like, which can be bought from the same source as the feathers.

Chief's headdress, fur, feathers, shell; Winnebago. Photograph courtesy of Milwaukee Public Museum.

The other materials can be picked up almost anywhere. Here, too, one should use what is at hand. The first war bonnets made by the author were of white turkey feathers dyed with leather dye and liquid shoe polish. Some war bonnets made of barred turkey feathers are worn by real Indians.

Full feather headdress; Chippewa. Photograph courtesy of Milwaukee Public Museum.

INDIAN   FEATHER   HEADDRESS

A simple hair ornament that can be made in one evening.

Any and all kinds of feathers can be worked into this headdress. If feathers look "scraggy", steam them over the spout of a teakettle.

To be worn on the back of the head.

Strip out this section

A few brightly dyed feathers or fluffs may be used

Individual taste enters into the making of this project, but some sort of balance should be maintained.

Fluff assembly added last. →

FRONT

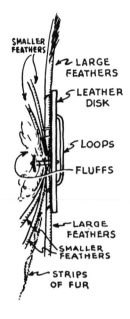

SMALLER FEATHERS

LARGE FEATHERS

LEATHER DISK

LOOPS

FLUFFS

LARGE FEATHERS

SMALLER FEATHERS

STRIPS OF FUR

Collect a bunch of different kinds of feathers: crow, owl, hawk chicken, turkey, etc. The more variety, the better. Bright feathers from game birds are excellent.

After the feathers are sewed onto the disk, a band of red or yellow cloth or a beaded band is slipped thru the loops and the job is done.

1
A 3 inch disk of sole leather. Punch 4 holes and fasten 2 loops of leather for headband to slip thru.

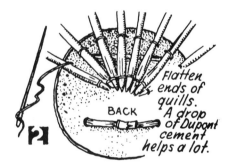

Flatten ends of quills. A drop of Dupont cement helps a lot.

BACK

2

Sew large quills all the way around. Punch holes with awl & use waxed cord.

3 Smaller feathers are next sewed on, and if a few strips of fur can be obtained, they should be added at this time.

4 Fasten some fluffs to a small leather disk and tie this assembly over the rest as shown above.

A SIOUAN
TURBAN
HEADDRESS

The headdress described here was sent to the author from the Black Hills as a token of friendship by Chief Wanblee Isnala (Lone Eagle) an Oglalla Sioux. It seemed a worthwhile project to pass on to lovers of Indian Lore.

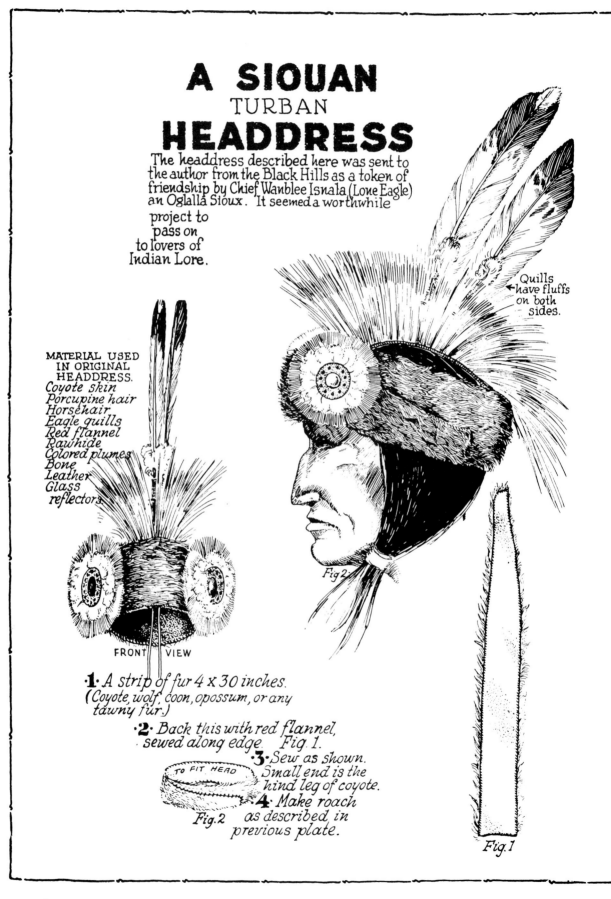

Quills have fluffs on both sides.

MATERIAL USED IN ORIGINAL HEADDRESS.
Coyote skin
Porcupine hair
Horsehair
Eagle quills
Red flannel
Rawhide
Colored plumes
Bone
Leather
Glass reflectors.

FRONT VIEW

Fig 2.

·1· A strip of fur 4 x 30 inches. (Coyote, wolf, coon, opossum, or any tawny fur.)

·2· Back this with red flannel, sewed along edge. Fig. 1.

·3· Sew as shown. Small end is the hind leg of coyote.

·4· Make roach as described in previous plate.

TO FIT HEAD

Fig. 2

Fig. 1

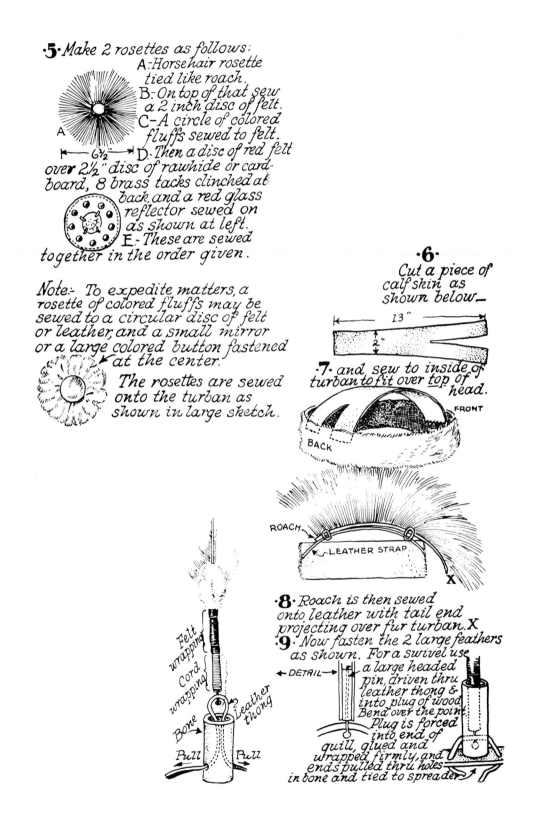

·5· Make 2 rosettes as follows:

A.- Horsehair rosette tied like roach.

B.- On top of that sew a 2 inch disc of felt.

C.- A circle of colored fluffs sewed to felt.

D.- Then a disc of red felt over 2½" disc of rawhide or cardboard, 8 brass tacks clinched at back, and a red glass reflector sewed on as shown at left.

E.- These are sewed together in the order given.

A

⟵ 6½" ⟶

Note:- To expedite matters, a rosette of colored fluffs may be sewed to a circular disc of felt or leather, and a small mirror or a large colored button fastened at the center.

The rosettes are sewed onto the turban as shown in large sketch.

·6· Cut a piece of calf skin as shown below—

13"

2"

·7· and sew to inside of turban to fit over top of head.

FRONT

BACK

ROACH

LEATHER STRAP

X

·8· Roach is then sewed onto leather with tail end projecting over fur turban. X

·9· Now fasten the 2 large feathers as shown. For a swivel use a large headed pin, driven thru leather thong & into plug of wood. Bend over the point. Plug is forced into end of quill, glued and wrapped firmly, and ends pulled thru holes in bone and tied to spreader.

Felt wrapping

Cord wrapping

Bone

Leather thong

Pull   Pull

⟵ DETAIL ⟶

INDIAN WAR BONNETS

War bonnets, or headdresses, as they are often called, can be made with barred turkey feathers. A strikingly attractive one can be made using black feathers with contrasting white fluffs. Short, wide feathers, about 8 or 10 inches long, may be made longer, as in Figure 1. (NOTE: The completed eagle feather shown in the plate below is 3 inches wide and 15 inches long.) Cut off the end of the quill and insert a smooth round stick, using cement glue to hold it (see Figure 1). When all the feathers have been prepared in this way, paint the sticks to match the quills.

Meanwhile, cut strips of leather 3/16 inch wide and 3 inches long, and get some fluffs that are about 8 inches long. Fasten the leather strips with adhesive tape as shown in Figure 2. A drop of cement may be used to secure the leather more permanently. Fasten the large fluff with the tape as shown in steps 7 and 8 on the plate, and finish as shown in step 9. Using white thread, tie the fluff to the feather. The thread will keep it in place on the stick. This method makes an attractive bonnet.

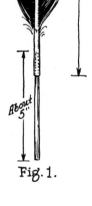

Fig. 1.

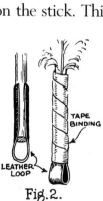

TAPE
BINDING

LEATHER
LOOP

Fig. 2.

Fig. 3.

≈ ELONGATED ≈
BLACK FEATHER
& WHITE FLUFFS

Hidatsa warrior, The Dog Dancer, Charles Bodmer, 1839. Photograph courtesy of Smithsonian Institution, National Museum of the American Indian.

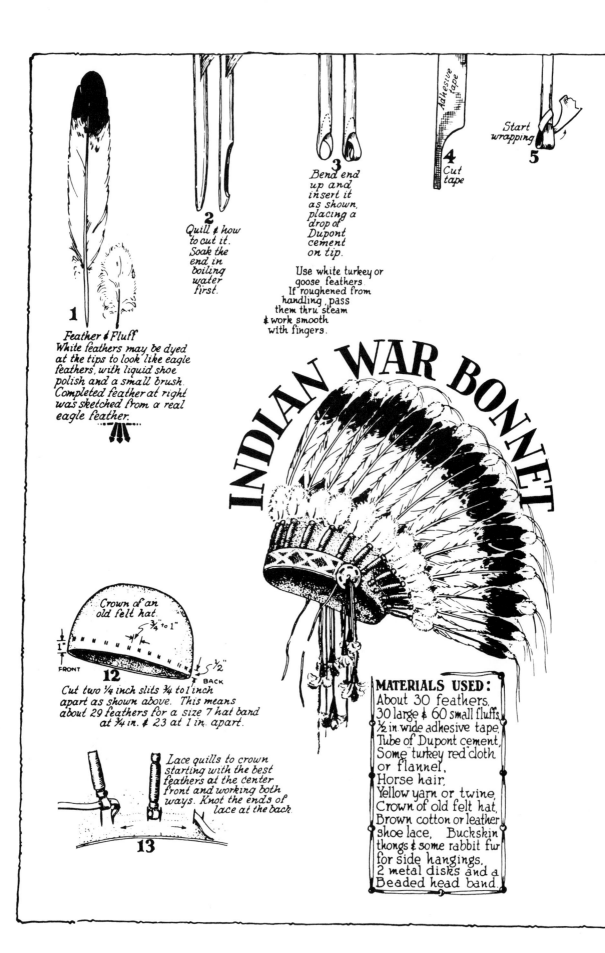

1

Feather & Fluff
White feathers may be dyed at the tips to look like eagle feathers, with liquid shoe polish and a small brush. Completed feather at right was sketched from a real eagle feather.

2

Quill & how to cut it. Soak the end in boiling water first.

3

Bend end up and insert it as shown, placing a drop of Dupont cement on tip.

Use white turkey or goose feathers. If roughened from handling, pass them thru steam & work smooth with fingers.

Adhesive tape

4
Cut tape

Start wrapping

5

INDIAN WAR BONNET

Crown of an old felt hat.

¾" to 1"

1"

FRONT

½"

BACK

12

Cut two ¼ inch slits ¾ to 1 inch apart as shown above. This means about 29 feathers for a size 7 hat band at ¾ in. & 23 at 1 in. apart.

Lace quills to crown starting with the best feathers at the center front and working both ways. Knot the ends of lace at the back.

13

MATERIALS USED:
About 30 feathers.
30 large & 60 small fluffs.
½ in. wide adhesive tape.
Tube of Dupont cement.
Some turkey red cloth or flannel.
Horse hair.
Yellow yarn or twine.
Crown of old felt hat.
Brown cotton or leather shoe lace. Buckskin thongs & some rabbit fur for side hangings.
2 metal disks and a Beaded head band.

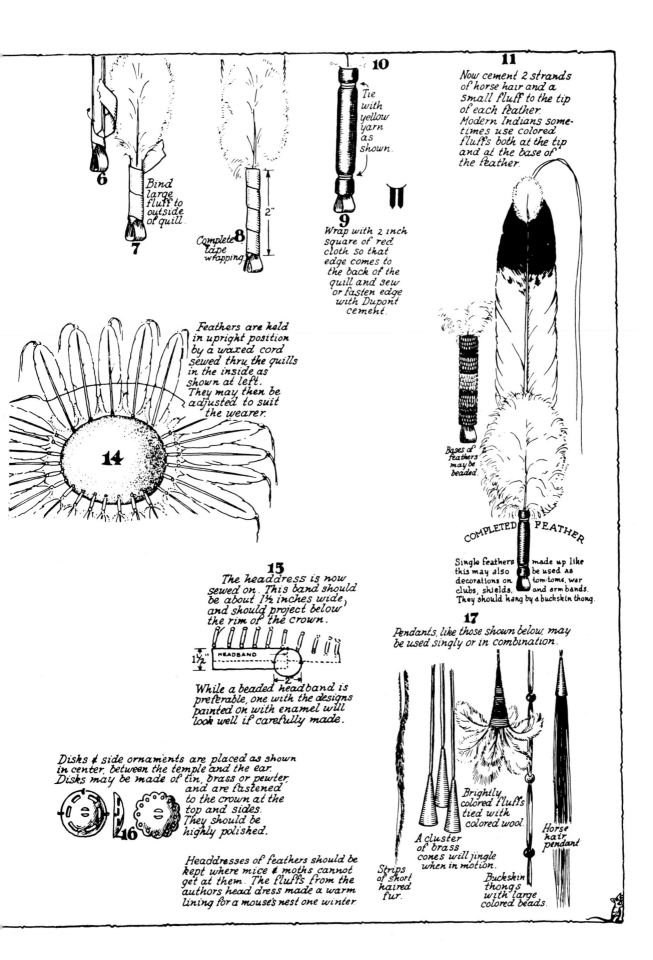

6

Bind large fluff to outside of quill.

7

Complete **8** tape wrapping.

2"

10

Tie with yellow yarn as shown.

9

Wrap with 2 inch square of red cloth so that edge comes to the back of the quill and sew or fasten edge with Dupont cement.

11

Now cement 2 strands of horse hair and a small fluff to the tip of each feather. Modern Indians sometimes use colored fluffs both at the tip and at the base of the feather.

Bases of feathers may be beaded.

COMPLETED FEATHER

Single feathers made up like this may also be used as decorations on tom-toms, war clubs, shields, and arm bands. They should hang by a buckskin thong.

Feathers are held in upright position by a waxed cord sewed thru the quills in the inside as shown at left. They may then be adjusted to suit the wearer.

14

15

The headdress is now sewed on. This band should be about 1½ inches wide, and should project below the rim of the crown.

HEADBAND

1½"

2"

While a beaded headband is preferable, one with the designs painted on with enamel will look well if carefully made.

17

Pendants, like those shown below, may be used singly or in combination.

Disks & side ornaments are placed as shown in center, between the temple and the ear. Disks may be made of tin, brass or pewter, and are fastened to the crown at the top and sides. They should be highly polished.

16

Headdresses of feathers should be kept where mice & moths cannot get at them. The fluffs from the authors head dress made a warm lining for a mouse's nest one winter.

Strips of short haired fur.

A cluster of brass cones will jingle when in motion.

Brightly colored fluffs tied with colored wool.

Buckskin thongs with large colored beads.

Horse hair pendant

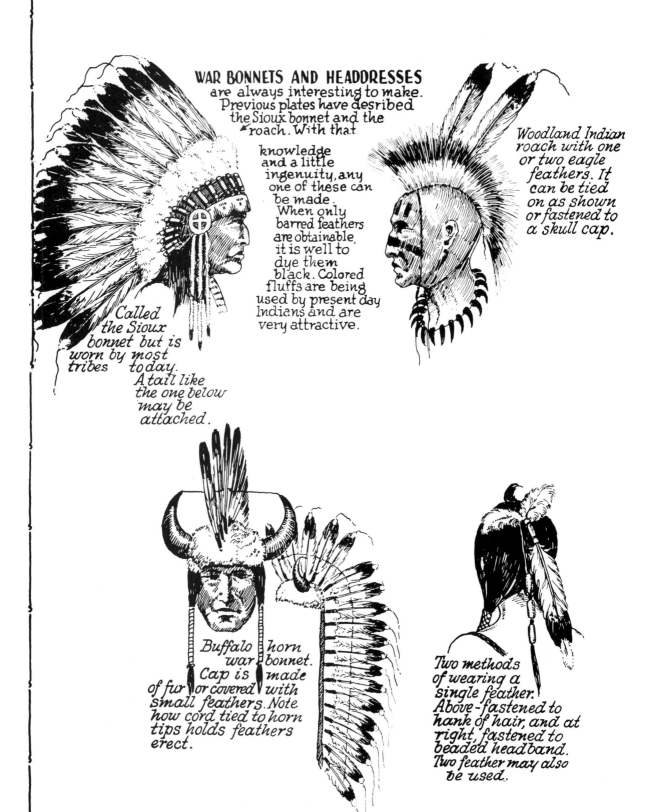

WAR BONNETS AND HEADDRESSES

are always interesting to make. Previous plates have desribed the Sioux bonnet and the roach. With that knowledge and a little ingenuity, any one of these can be made.

When only barred feathers are obtainable, it is well to dye them black. Colored fluffs are being used by present day Indians and are very attractive.

Called the Sioux bonnet but is worn by most tribes today. A tail like the one below may be attached.

Woodland Indian roach with one or two eagle feathers. It can be tied on as shown or fastened to a skull cap.

Buffalo horn war bonnet. Cap is made of fur or covered with small feathers. Note how cord tied to horn tips holds feathers erect.

Two methods of wearing a single feather. Above - fastened to hank of hair, and at right, fastened to beaded headband. Two feather may also be used.

A wig to resemble the above sketch can be made by sewing manila or sisal fiber to a skull cap. Dye the fiber and sew it on while moist.

Blackfoot headdress.

Iroquois headdress. Also worn by other woodland Indians.

Plain band worn by Pueblos and Navajos Usually red.

Use a skull cap for the base.

Mandan headdress made of barred tail feathers and curled breast feathers from any large fowl.

INDIAN NECKLACES

Indians made necklaces out of anything that came their way—bone, copper and brass tubing, beads of all kinds, bear, eagle, and mountain lion claws, and the like. Grizzly bear claws were highly prized because life was endangered in getting them. A necklace of matched claws was something to be proud of! A necklace of wooden claws is described.
The beads are made of wood, painted blue.
Smaller black glass beads are placed between the larger beads.

A necklace made from the wing bones of ducks and chickens is shown in the photograph. These small bones are cleaned, boiled to remove the grease, cut to size, and rubbed smooth with fine sandpaper. Corncob pipe stems also can be used for this type of necklace.

If possible, these necklaces should be strung with thin buckskin thongs.

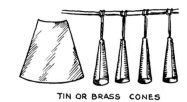

SHEEP TOES

22 CAL CARTRIDGE SHELLS

TIN OR BRASS CONES

Fig. 1

Fig. 2

Fig. 3

Indians in ceremonial dress and paint at 4th of July celebration, 1905;
Plains. Photograph courtesy of Milwaukee Public Museum.

BEAR CLAW NECKLACE

Bear claw necklaces are very highly prized by all Indians lucky enough to acquire one and in these days when grizzly bears are getting rather scarce, bear claws are often made of bone, horn or wood. By following these instructions you can make bear claws of wood that will almost deceive an expert.

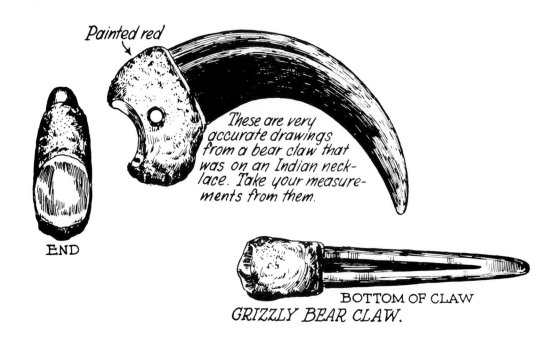

Painted red

These are very accurate drawings from a bear claw that was on an Indian necklace. Take your measurements from them.

END

BOTTOM OF CLAW

GRIZZLY BEAR CLAW.

THIS IS HOW THEY ACTUALLY LOOK.
Use side views for templates

Paint red or orange.

These drawings are from a
BLACK BEAR CLAW.

Indians trim away the hair from the base of the claw, leaving the bone in the claw. The bone is painted and the claw is scraped and polished.

THIS IS HOW TO WHITTLE THEM

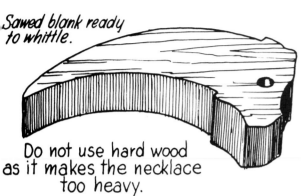

Sawed blank ready to whittle.

Do not use hard wood as it makes the necklace too heavy.

1 Cut a paper template the size and shape of the claw you wish to use.

2 Then lay out about 10 or 12 on a ⅝ inch board. Basswood is best but any soft wood will do.

3 Saw out the blanks and drill holes.

4 Whittle to shape with pocketknife and work smooth with a file or sandpaper.

5 Finish the claw proper with fine sandpaper. The base should look like bone and should not be finished too smoothly.

THIS IS HOW TO GIVE THEM A NATURALISTIC FINISH

Finish the base with hot paraffin also.

First paint the base with red paint, either thin oil paint or water color and allow to dry. Then blacken the claw part over a candle flame. Dip it in the hot paraffin from time to time and rub the paraffin well into the wood with your fingers, until the claw is quit dark. Be careful not to blacken the painted part. When it gets to be a dark brown or black overall, let it cool and with fine sandpaper rub down the upper part of the claw to lighten the color as show in upper sketch. Black bear claws are shaded just the opposite. Then rub in some more hot paraffin, let cool and polish with a cloth until they shine.

PUMP DRILLS

Pump drills and bow drills are clumsy and ineffective tools, yet Indians and Eskimos make good use of them, even today.

Years ago, while visiting the Zuñi Indians in the southwestern part of our country, I saw a wonderful turquoise necklace made by a Zuñi Indian worth between $700 and $1,000. The necklace was made of about 30 or 40 individual strings, each of which consisted of many fine turquoise beads. The beads on each of the strings were shaped differently. There were spherical, tubular, and flat round beads. There were also turquoise pieces cut into animal shapes. Some were as small as ⅛ inch in diameter, and from ¹⁄₁₆ to ³⁄₁₆ inches long. Some of the tubular beads were ¼ inch in diameter and from ⅜ to ½ inches long. Some of the spherical beads were ⅛ inch in diameter, but there were also some as large as ¼ inch. The animal and bird shaped beads were made of pieces of turquoise approximately ½ by ¾ by 1 inch.

All of the thousands of pieces of turquoise used on these 30 or 40 strings in the necklace had been carefully drilled by a patient Indian craftsman, who used the crudest of tools, among them a pump drill.

Chief Nana in costume; Apache. Photograph courtesy of Smithsonian
Institution, National Museum of the American Indian.

A PUMP DRILL

The pump drill is at one and the same time, an ancient, a modern and a handy tool. It was and is still used by Indians and other craftsmen for shell, coral, turquois and other material. The fact that it can be operated with one hand leaving the other to hold the material to be drilled, makes it worth having.

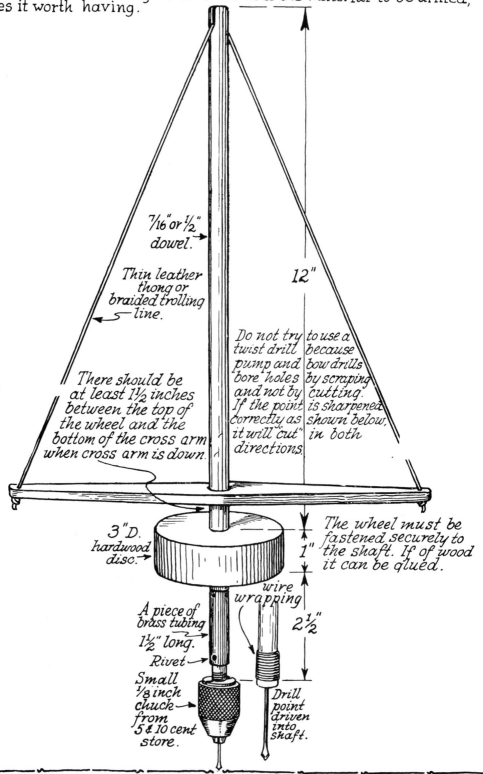

7/16" or 1/2" dowel.

Thin leather thong or braided trolling line.

There should be at least 1½ inches between the top of the wheel and the bottom of the cross arm when cross arm is down.

12"

Do not try to use a twist drill pump and bore holes and not by If the point correctly as it will cut directions.

to use a because bow drills by scraping cutting. is sharpened shown below, in both

3" D. hardwood disc.

The wheel must be fastened securely to the shaft. If of wood it can be glued.

1"

wire wrapping

2½"

A piece of brass tubing 1½" long.

Rivet

Small 1/8 inch chuck from 5 & 10 cent store.

Drill point driven into shaft.

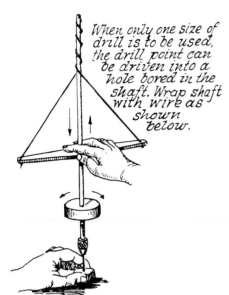

When only one size of drill is to be used, the drill point can be driven into a hole bored in the shaft. Wrap shaft with wire as shown below.

TO OPERATE A PUMP DRILL, give the shaft a few turns as shown above & press down. The momentum will rewind the cord, the cross arm going up at the same time. Then press down again. Just keep pumping.

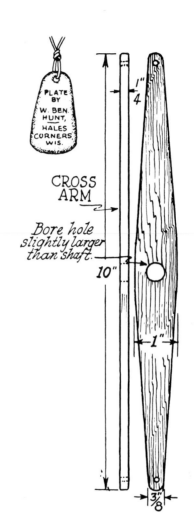

PLATE BY W. BEN. HUNT, HALES CORNERS WIS.

CROSS ARM

Bore hole slightly larger than shaft.

1"/4

10"

1"

3"/8

A small metal wheel with the correct bore may be used.

To fasten chuck to shaft, file the shank of chuck to fit snugly into brass tubing. Drill thru tubing and shank and rivet with a section of wire nail. Then trim shaft to fit into upper end of tubing and fasten with punch pricks or drill thru and rivet with small brad.

DRILL POINTS should be made of good steel. Pieces of knitting or heavy darning needles make good points. Heat end to cherry red and hammer flat. Then shape as shown below. Now heat it again & plunge it into cold water to harden it.

Enlarged View.

Sharpen from both sides.

HINTS ON WORKING WITH BONE

Indians and Eskimos make use of bone in many ways; and bone, when carefully treated and worked, looks very much like ivory. Once you get to working with bone you will always keep an eye on the kitchen to see that good bones are not thrown away.

Bones that have been in the oven, or that have been cooked, may be rather greasy. Cut off the parts not wanted with a hacksaw. Then scrape off all scraps of meat and clean the marrow out of the bone.

There are two methods of bleaching cooked bones. One is to boil them, being careful to place something on the bottom of the kettle, so that the bones do not rest on it, or otherwise they may turn brown. A safer method is to let them stand in warm water for a day or two. A kettle on the back of the stove, in which water may be kept at a warm temperature, will do very nicely for this purpose.

Raw bones require a different treatment. Scrape them and remove the marrow and put them in the sun to bleach, or better still, place them on an ant hill. You may be sure that the ants will clean them thoroughly.

Bone can easily be cut and scraped with a knife. For a fine finish, rub with fine sandpaper or Carborundum paper or cloth, and then polish with a coarse cloth and linseed oil.

Holes may be drilled with a knife point, or with a pump drill.

When bone is to be engraved, it should be done before it is polished, as this lessens the chance of the tool slipping. A sharp-pointed awl is excellent for engraving bone. To color the engraved lines, follow the lines with a pen and waterproof ink or with a colored indelible lead pencil. Then go over them with very fine sandpaper and polish with cloth.

Turtle bone and glass necklace; Sioux. Photograph courtesy of Milwaukee Public Museum.

INDIAN "BONE" BREASTPLATE

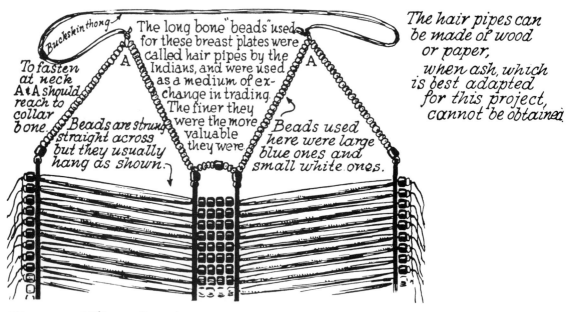

Buckskin thong

To fasten at neck A+A should reach to collar bone.

The long bone "beads" used for these breast plates were called hair pipes by the Indians, and were used as a medium of exchange in trading. The finer they were the more valuable they were.

A

A

Beads are strung straight across but they usually hang as shown.

Beads used here were large blue ones and small white ones.

The hair pipes can be made of wood or paper, when ash, which is best adapted for this project, cannot be obtained.

There are 94 "bones" in the breastplate shown here. The bone section measures 12 inches from top to bottom.

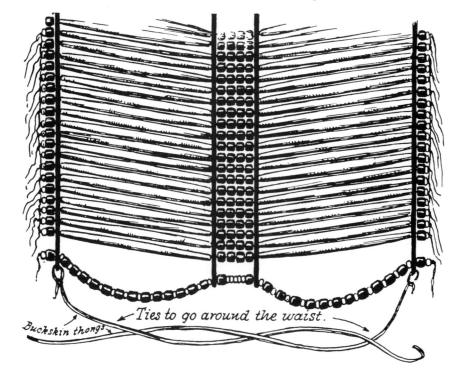

Ties to go around the waist.

Buckskin thong

1

TO MAKE THEM OF WOOD *cut a bundle of green ash shoots (not branches) ³/8" thick*

2

Cut out the sections between buds or branches. Fig.1. Indians made hair pipes from 3 to 5½ inches long.

3

Poke out pithy core with a stiff wire as shown in Fig.2.

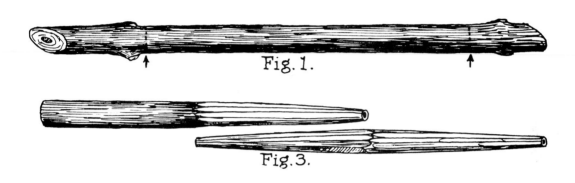

Fig. 1.

Fig. 3.

File the end of the wire straight across so that the core is pushed out ahead of it.

4

Now sharpen your knife to a good keen edge and whittle first one half to shape, and then the other, Fig. 3. to about ¼ inch in the middle and tapering down to about ⁵/32 inch at the ends. This calls for some very careful whittling and a very sharp pocket knife.

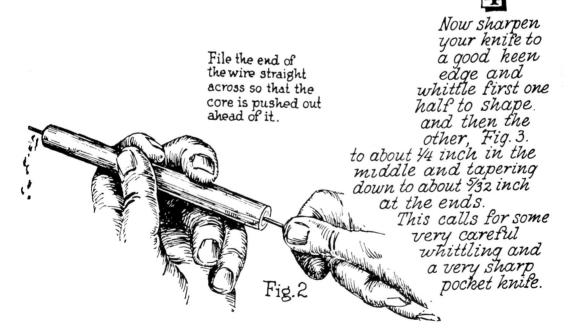

Fig.2

5 Now scrape down the high spots with the sharp edge of your knife and smoothen with fine sandpaper   Fig. 4 shows a finished "hair pipe" ⟶

←Fig. 4.

6 Then rub them with a rag dipped in a mixture of boiled linseed oil and raw sienna which gives them a bonelike appearance.

7 While they are drying, cut 4 strips of thick leather about 13 or 14 inches long and ⅜ inch wide.

8 Mark off the holes evenly down the center, spacing them so that when the hair pipes are strung they will almost touch each other. Use an awl or a small nail for punching the holes, and punch the strips exactly alike.

9 Large beads may be round ⊙ or tubular, ⊙ of glass, or wood, and any suitable color. Brass beads look dandy. They should be about the same diameter as the thickest part of the hair pipes. The small beads should be of a contrasting color.

10 Use waxed carpet warp, linen, or any other stout cord for tying. Tie a knot at the end of the string and thread in the order shown, tying the end of each string around the previous string end. See that each row is quite taut.

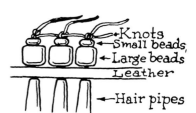

←Knots
←Small beads
←Large beads
Leather
←Hair pipes

HOW TO MAKE THEM OF PAPER

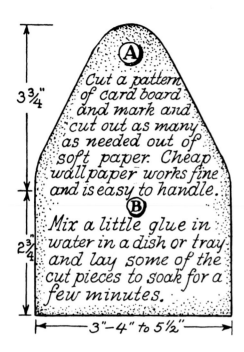

3¾"

Ⓐ Cut a pattern of card board and mark and cut out as many as needed out of soft paper. Cheap wall paper works fine and is easy to handle.

Ⓑ Mix a little glue in water in a dish or tray and lay some of the cut pieces to soak for a few minutes.

2¾"

← 3"–4" to 5½" →

Note: If lighter paper is used, add an inch or two to the length, making the upper section 4¾" & the lower section 3¾"

Ⓒ Then, starting at the wide end, wrap one around a piece of straight wire. Roll it with your hand as shown below until it forms a tight firm roll. Wipe off with dry cloth.

Ⓓ Remove wire and allow "bones" to dry

Ⓔ Then sandpaper very carefully to take down edges.

Ⓕ Give them a thin coat of shellac

Ⓖ Rub smooth with fine steel wool or sandpaper and give them a coat of ivory or light cream colored enamel preferably with an eggshell finish. Paper "bones" make a light weight breastplate with evenly matched "bones"

Ⓗ The method of assembling is the same as the one with wooden "bones."

Almost any combination of "bones" & beads may be used.

BONE & SHELL NECKLACE

This necklace was made of the small wing-bones of ducks chickens and geese, a piece of clam shell and a few beads. It is very attractive and easy to make.

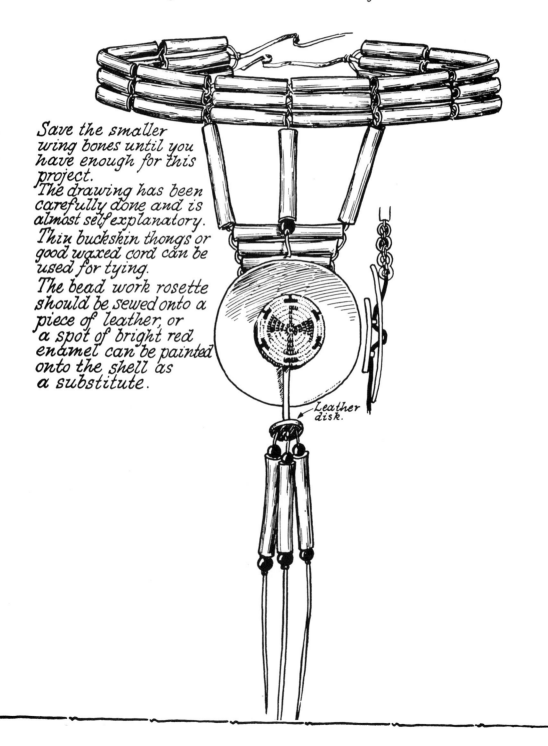

Save the smaller wing bones until you have enough for this project.

The drawing has been carefully done and is almost self explanatory.

Thin buckskin thongs or good waxed cord can be used for tying.

The bead work rosette should be sewed onto a piece of leather, or a spot of bright red enamel can be painted onto the shell as a substitute.

Leather disk.

A BONE
NECKERCHIEF SLIDE

This slide is made from a section of leg-of-lamb bone, and when nicely made resembles Eskimo ivory work.

Cut out this section with a hack saw.

2½"

Drill holes & finish with knife & file.

TOP VIEW

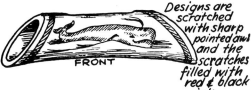

FRONT

Designs are scratched with sharp pointed awl and the scratches filled with red & black ink.

BACK.

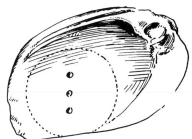

Cut a circular disk out of a clam shell with a coping saw. File the edge smooth and drill the three holes with a pump drill. A disk of polished tin or brass may be used instead of shell.

A NATURAL BONE
NECKERCHIEF SLIDE

The slide shown here is a ready-made one that requires very little trimming. It is found fastened to the base of the skull of deer, sheep, goats, etc., and can easily be sawed off. Your butcher should be able to get some of them for you.

These bones look very much like skulls of Big Horn sheep.

Saw cut.

BACK

BOTTOM

•[READ OPPOSITE PAGE FOR TREATMENT OF BONES]

MEDICINE POLES OR OWNERSHIP STAFFS

The Mandans, a tribe of Plains Indians who lived on the upper Missouri River, used a medicine pole in the same manner that the West Coast Indians used a totem pole, except that the medicine pole was not stationary. It was taken inside at night and in bad weather. Each owner decorated his medicine pole to suit his individual taste.

Today, this idea can be carried out in two ways: each "Indian" may make his own individual medicine pole, or a group pole can be made for each tepee or wigwam. On the tepee pole, which would belong to 4 to 6 persons, each should contribute his skill or creativity. Use plenty of color. Paint as well as colored cloth may be used to brighten these poles. For the top part, a small piece of buckskin or chamois skin should be used inside the loop. The symbol or design of the tepee may be put on this with pen and ink or with paint. Brown ball-point ink is just the thing for decorating buckskin; this ink makes the design appear as though it had been burned in with a red-hot wire.

LANCES

In the days when the Indians still fought for their hunting grounds, the Plains Indians, who usually had horses, used lances for close fighting. After Indians had guns, the lances were only used for ceremonial purposes. The average Indian craftsman, with enough feathers for a fine lance, would probably rather make a war bonnet. But when he has a war bonnet and some extra feathers, the feathered lance is an attractive part of his outfit.

Group on horseback, left to right: 1) ————, 2) ————, 3) Plenty Coups, 4) Wet, 5) Wolf Eating, 6) Bull Don't Fall Down, 7) John Wallace, 8) Spotted Rabbit, 9) Big Snake, 10) Plain Owl, 11) Smart Enemy, 12) Holds Enemy. Photo by W. Wildschut, 1910, courtesy of Smithsonian Institution, National Museum of the American Indian.

CEREMONIAL LANCES

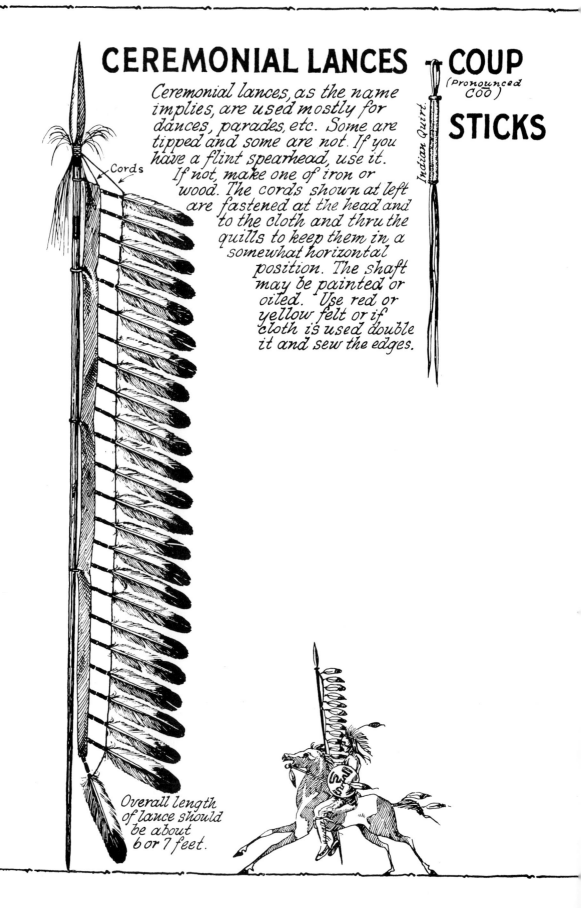

Ceremonial lances, as the name implies, are used mostly for dances, parades, etc. Some are tipped and some are not. If you have a flint spearhead, use it. If not, make one of iron or wood. The cords shown at left are fastened at the head and to the cloth and thru the quills to keep them in a somewhat horizontal position. The shaft may be painted or oiled. Use red or yellow felt or if cloth is used double it and sew the edges.

Cords

COUP
(Pronounced COO)

STICKS

Indian Quirt.

Overall length of lance should be about 6 or 7 feet.

Coup sticks were used by warriors to strike an enemy. It was considered a great honor to "count coup" on an enemy, and more so if the enemy was not wounded at the time. Make them as shown using strips of fur or red cloth to wrap the stick, or use both. Use feathers and horse hair for decorations.

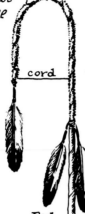

cord

Red cloth →

Any short-haired fur will do. Cut it in strips and wrap it spirally. Do the same with the red cloth.

An Indian could "count coup" with his bow, his quirt, or in fact with any thing at all, but a well equipped warrior carried his coup stick. Make it about 5 or 6 feet long. Bend the crook while green and let it dry. A cord tied as shown, will keep it in shape.

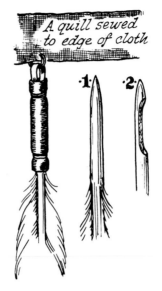

A quill sewed to edge of cloth

·1· ·2·

Soak quill in hot water— then cut and bend. (3 & 4)

·3· ·4· ·5· ·6·

Tape

Cut tape like this.

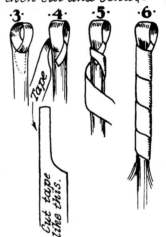

·7·

Prepare feathers as for war bonnet, but leave out the fluffs. Use red cloth → for final wrapping, glue edge, and tie with yellow cord →

OWNERSHIP STAFFS

Tin cones

Horse hair or fiber

Short fur

Stripped feathers

Long fur

Fluff pendants

Halves of large feathers

Tin cones or cartridge shells

Pointed to set in hole

The staffs shown on this page are not Indian in the strict sense of the word, altho they have certain Indian characteristics They are meant to be stuck into the ground in front of cabins, wigwams, or tepees to tell which "Indians" live within They also help to brighten up the area Make them of saplings 8 or 9 feet long. They are laid out in sections of 10 or 12 inches, and each is carved and decorated section to suit himself. A few suggestions are shown here. For material use fur, feathers, leather, buckskin, red cloth, tin cones, empty cartridge shells, and some oil paints.

Tin Cone

Fluffs tied to leather thong and pulled up into cone

Brass upholsterer's tacks can be used for ornamentation or to fasten leather, etc.

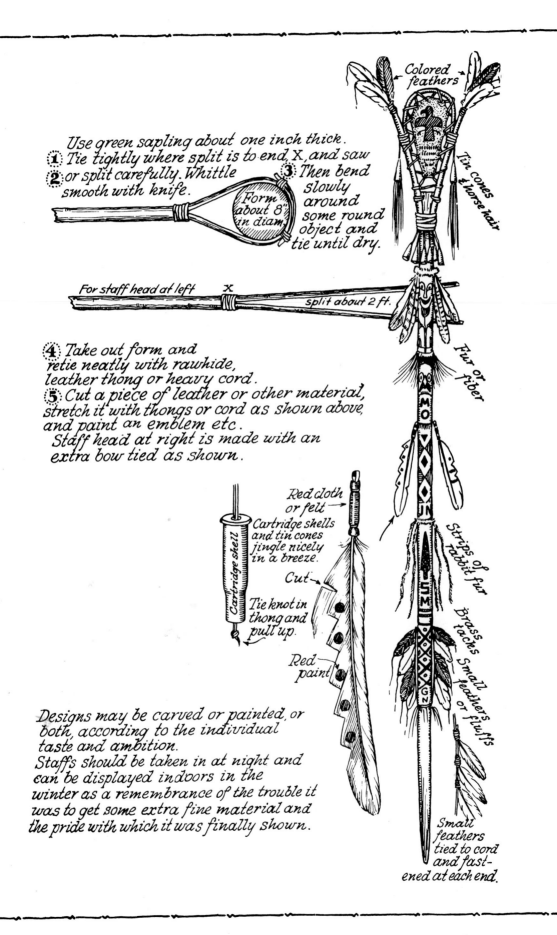

Use green sapling about one inch thick.
①Tie tightly where split is to end, X, and saw
②or split carefully. Whittle smooth with knife.
③Then bend slowly around some round object and tie until dry.

Form about 8" in diam.

Colored feathers

Tin cones & horse hair

For staff head at left   X   split about 2 ft.

Fur or fiber

④Take out form and retie neatly with rawhide, leather thong or heavy cord.
⑤Cut a piece of leather or other material, stretch it with thongs or cord as shown above, and paint an emblem etc.
Staff head at right is made with an extra bow tied as shown.

Red cloth or felt →
Cartridge shells and tin cones jingle nicely in a breeze.

Cartridge shell

Cut →

Tie knot in thong and pull up.

Red paint

Strips of rabbit fur

Brass tacks

Small feathers or fluffs

Designs may be carved or painted, or both, according to the individual taste and ambition.
Staffs should be taken in at night and can be displayed indoors in the winter as a remembrance of the trouble it was to get some extra fine material and the pride with which it was finally shown.

Small feathers tied to cord and fastened at each end.

WHITTLING

Although the definition of whittling is "cutting away the surface of wood with a knife," to me it means using a pocketknife to make any project that requires material that can be cut with a knife. In other words, it is the ability to use a knife effectively. Whittling tools must be kept very sharp.

The best woods for whittling are softwoods. One of the nicest is green basswood. Kachina dolls, peace pipes, awl handles, and many other things can be whittled easily from green basswood. Whittling a lacrosse stick or a pack rack with a hand ax and a pocketknife can be more satisfying than making a fine chair with power tools.

It takes practice, however, to become really skillful with either ax or pocketknife. Just to be able to trim down a half-inch stick for a cane and do a neat job of trimming off the branches may be a hard job for the beginner. Do not use a knife for every kind of work. Where large things are to be made of wood, it would be foolish to do it with a jackknife when other tools are handy. But there are times when it is useful to know how to whittle. There are times when a certain tool is badly needed; being skillful with a knife is very valuable at such times.

Echo mask; British Columbia. Photograph courtesy of Milwaukee
Public Museum.

WHITTLING

Whittling means cutting away the surface of wood with a knife. The best knife for ordinary whittling is a 2 or 3 bladed pocketknife with a handle measuring about 3½ inches long. It should have one large strong blade and 1 or 2 small blades, as shown on opposite page. The best woods for whittling are white pine, bass, cottonwood, cedar, poplar and willow. Do not use sandpaper to finish a whittled article, as much of the beauty of a good piece of whittling lies in the pattern of the knife cuts.

Arrows show direction in which to cut

Cut "with the grain" to prevent knife from digging into the wood at the wrong place. If the wood does not show the grain, the knife will find it.

A good position for ordinary whittling.

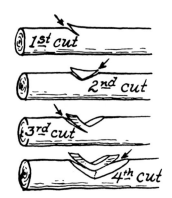

Method of cutting notches. Trying to cut too deep in one cut is likely to split the wood.

1st cut

2nd cut

3rd cut

4th cut

134

Always hold your knife with a firm grip and cut away from yourself whenever possible.

Sketch at right shows how wood and knife should be held when making long cuts or when trimming branches

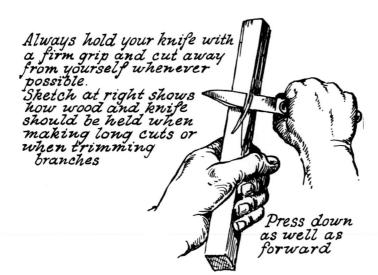

Press down as well as forward

TRIMMING SMALL BRANCHES

Direction of grain in branch and twig.

Make first cut toward the upper end and —

the second downward.

To cut through a piece of wood, start as shown at left, making a series of V-cuts all the way around (1st & 2nd cut) then make a larger cut, (3rd & 4th cut) and so on, until through as shown above! The ends may then be trimmed as shown below. Upper end of piece should be trimmed like this.

WHITTLING

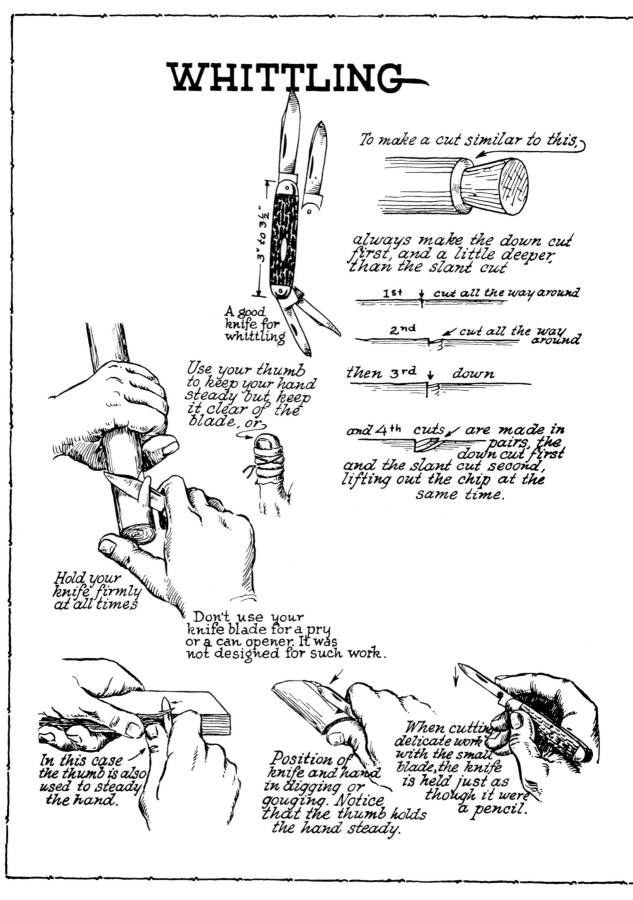

A good knife for whittling

3" to 3½"

To make a cut similar to this,

always make the down cut first, and a little deeper, than the slant cut

1st ↓ cut all the way around

2nd ↙ cut all the way around

then 3rd ↓ down

and 4th cuts ↙ are made in pairs, the down cut first and the slant cut second, lifting out the chip at the same time.

Use your thumb to keep your hand steady but keep it clear of the blade, or

Hold your knife firmly at all times

Don't use your knife blade for a pry or a can opener. It was not designed for such work.

In this case the thumb is also used to steady the hand.

Position of knife and hand in digging or gouging. Notice that the thumb holds the hand steady.

When cutting delicate work with the small blade, the knife is held just as though it were a pencil.

136

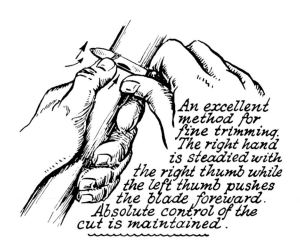

An excellent method for fine trimming. The right hand is steadied with the right thumb while the left thumb pushes the blade foreward. Absolute control of the cut is maintained.

♦ THREE GOOD KNIVES ♦
THAT COME IN HANDY.

A sloyd knife. No danger of blade closing while whittling.

A skew-bladed knife comes in handy where much downward cutting is required.

Cutting edge

The Indians use a curved blade for gouging out bowls & ladles.

A FEW GOOD RULES
TO BEAR IN MIND.

Always keep knife blades sharp and clean.

Never lay your knife down. Close it and put it in your pocket, and you'll always know where it is.

Don't try to whittle hard wood or wood containing resin.

The edge of a good blade should not chip or bend over with ordinary usage.

On a camping trip, take a whetstone along, as you can always find water, whereas there never seems to be any oil around for an oil stone.

In a pinch, a knife can be sharpened on a piece of fine emery cloth laid on a flat surface.

Don't use a pocket knife to open cans, to scrape metal or for prying things open or apart.

And remember—it shows poor manners to carve initials in other people's trees or property.

FALSE FACES AND MASKS

The false faces shown here are imitations of the heavy wood masks which were carved by members of the false-face societies among the Iroquois Indian tribes.

The false-face societies were secret organizations. Membership could be achieved by dreaming about the masks, or about the society's ceremonials. Information about the dream had to be given to the proper person; and after an initiation feast was given, membership was established. Leaving the society was just as simple. Dream about no longer being a member, report this, and give a farewell feast.

The members of these societies wore these masks while trying to cure the sick, alleviate pain, exorcise witches, or drive out demons.

The Iroquois were a federation of the Seneca, Oneida, Onondaga, Mohawk, and Cayuga tribes. The Seneca were probably the first to have societies of this kind, but the other four tribes were also acquainted with them, and their rites are still observed among the eastern Iroquois.

The false faces shown may be altered to suit various tastes. They make excellent wall decorations.

False Face mask; Iroquois. Photograph courtesy of Milwaukee
Public Museum.

FALSE FACES and MASKS

False faces have been made and used by almost every class of civilized and savage people. Indians, Eskimos and some African tribes carve very interesting false faces of wood. They are usually hollowed out to fit over the dancer's face during ceremonial dances. False faces and masks are not difficult to make and are interesting whittling and carving projects. The backs may be left solid and they may be used for ornamental purposes. Soft, light woods, such as pine, poplar, bass, cottonwood and willow are usually used, and are easily carved.

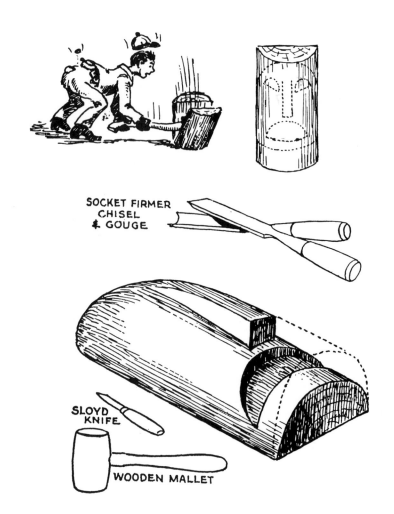

SOCKET FIRMER
CHISEL
& GOUGE

SLOYD
KNIFE

WOODEN MALLET

·1· Get a piece of wood about 6 inches wide, 2½ to 3 inches thick and about 15 inches long. This allows space for clamping to bench or saw horse while carving.

·2· Trim off rough and uneven places and pencil out top curve, nose, and mouth.

·3· Shape top first, then cut down at sides and bottom of nose, and cut away surplus wood. Round it smoothly.

·4· Then lay out mouth again. cut straight down about ⅜ or ½ inch and take out as shown leaving a smooth bottom surface. (Left.)

·5· Lay out eyes, lines above mouth and on forehead

·6· Cut out the eyes according to section drawing at left.

·7· Now carve the hair line on forehead and the line over the mouth as shown below.

For bookends make them ⅔ size (right)

Section showing how eye is cut out

·8· Cut the teeth as shown, using V cuts for the up and down cuts and an inward slant cut at the bottom of the teeth.

·9· The lower part which was left on for clamping is cut off last.

These false faces are usually finished very smoothly and painted, sometimes in only one color, and sometimes in two or more colors. A mate to this one, smiling, with a base added would make a pair of book ends.

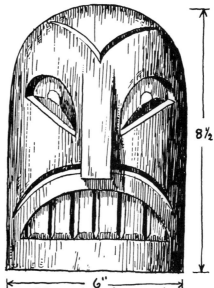

8½

6"
Dimensions for mask.

141

FALSE FACES and MASKS

may be made anywhere from 1 inch high to life size depending upon the material available and the ambition of the craftsman. If used for a wall decoration, bore a slanting ½ inch hole into the back, on the center-line, near the top, and hang as shown

IROQUOIS
FALSE FACE

WISCONSIN
ONEIDA

Both of
these masks
are painted a reddish
brown and most Iroquois
false faces have pieces of tin
or brass with holes in them for eyes.

These small sketches are about the actual size of the original. There was a cord attached and it was probably worn as a badge to show that the warrior was a member of the Iroquois False face Society. These small masks are a lot of fun and can be made with nothing more than a sharp, small-bladed pocket knife.

142

**IROQUOIS
FALSE FACE**

The false faces and masks shown on this plate are from sketches made at the Milwaukee Public Museum and are some of the most interesting ones. They are shown here to show what Indians can do with a very few tools, probably with only a knife of some sort.

The plate on the opposite page shows the simplest kind of mask carving and the same method can be used in making more elaborate ones.

The mask shown below is very attractive and is not difficult to make. A triangular billet is cut as shown → and most of the carving is done on the two flat sides. Careful painting helps a lot in making this one.

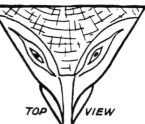

TOP VIEW

W — WHITE
R — RED
B — BLUE
THE REST IS BLACK
**THUNDERBIRD MASK
FROM BRITISH COLUMBIA**

RED LINE

NECKERCHIEF SLIDES

A lot of fun can be had whittling this type of neckerchief slide. The piece of wood, out of which the slide is whittled, is small enough to carry in a pocket. At home, or on a hike, or at any other time, it can be worked on for the few minutes which otherwise would be wasted. Many different designs can be worked out using the same general principle. Figures 1, 2, and 3 show a few designs. If the whittler is clever he can carve his slide so that it need not be painted at all. Basswood is ideal for small carvings of this kind. It is tough enough, has a fine grain, and is easy to cut.

When working out a different design, it is a good idea to make a rough sketch on paper first.

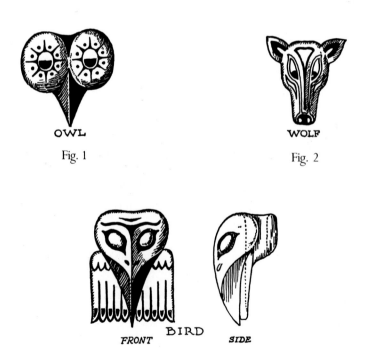

OWL

Fig. 1

WOLF

Fig. 2

FRONT BIRD SIDE

Fig. 3

Man, Chief Mountain, in costume; Blackfoot. Photograph courtesy of
Smithsonian Institution, National Museum of the American Indian.

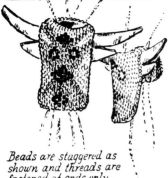

Beads are staggered as shown and threads are fastened at ends only.

·NECKERCHIEF· ·····SLIDES····

The slides shown at the left & right were made by Indians. The structural parts of these slides are neck vertebræ of sheep and cows. A little whittling forms the horns and ears. The head proper is then covered with cloth or thin buckskin and then covered with beadwork. These vertebræ are rather scarce, because when animals are butchered by white men, they are split down the full length of the backbone, thus splitting these vertebræ. But we can whittle these cows head slides of wood, paint them carefully and have something unique in about one quarter of the time it takes an Indian to make a beaded one.

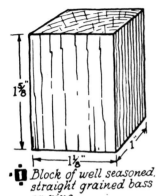

· **1** · Block of well seasoned, straight grained bass or pine.

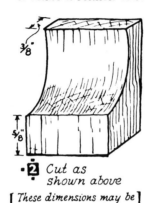

· **2** · Cut as shown above

[These dimensions may be changed slightly.]

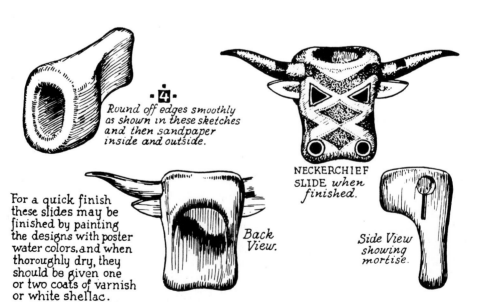

· **4** · Round off edges smoothly as shown in these sketches and then sandpaper inside and outside.

For a quick finish these slides may be finished by painting the designs with poster water colors, and when thoroughly dry, they should be given one or two coats of varnish or white shellac.

NECKERCHIEF SLIDE when finished.

Back View.

Side View showing mortise.

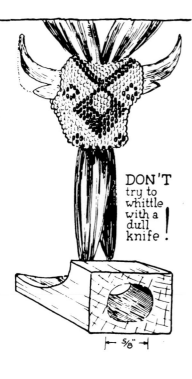

DON'T try to whittle with a dull knife!

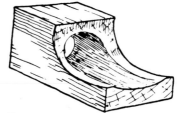

·3 With the small blade of a pocket knife whittle out the hole as shown above. Do not try to bore it out with a bit as it is apt to split the block. 3 or 4 small holes may be made with a ¼" drill and then the remainder whittled out.

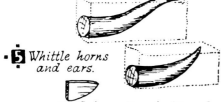

·5 Whittle horns and ears.

·6 Cut mortises to fit and glue them in place.

For a durable finish use enamel or lacquer. Any bright color may be used depending on individual taste. Both inside and outside should be painted to prevent moisture from causing subsequent splitting

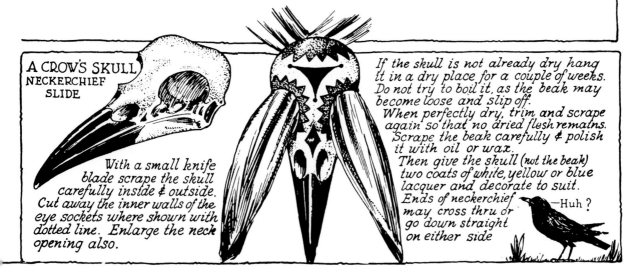

A CROW'S SKULL NECKERCHIEF SLIDE

With a small knife blade scrape the skull carefully inside & outside. Cut away the inner walls of the eye sockets where shown with dotted line. Enlarge the neck opening also.

If the skull is not already dry hang it in a dry place for a couple of weeks. Do not try to boil it, as the beak may become loose and slip off.
When perfectly dry, trim and scrape again so that no dried flesh remains. Scrape the beak carefully & polish it with oil or wax.
Then give the skull (not the beak) two coats of white, yellow or blue lacquer and decorate to suit.
Ends of neckerchief may cross thru or go down straight on either side

—Huh?

INDIAN PEACE PIPES

Peace pipes, or calumets as they are also called, were used by the Indians in councils. Smoking a peace pipe was a sign that the smoker gave his pledge of honor. It was thought that the smoke made one think more clearly. For this reason the pipe was always passed around to everyone before a treaty was even talked about.

Peace pipes were always held sacred by the Indians. They were never laid upon the ground, and when not in use were kept in an ornamented buckskin pipe bag.

The stems were decorated with horsehair, fur, feathers, plumes, colored cloth, and paint.

Use your own ideas in designing the bowl, carving animals or birds, or the heads of animals or birds, on the bowl proper or at the front or back of the bowl.

Pipes of the kind described may also be made of Mexican pottery clay, but these must be handled more carefully than the ones made of wood.

Indian pipe; Iowa. Photograph courtesy of Milwaukee Public Museum.

INDIAN PEACE PIPES

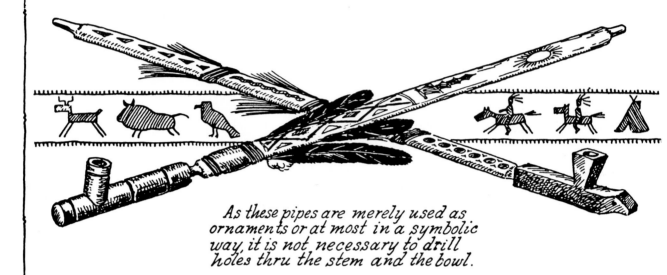

As these pipes are merely used as
ornaments or at most in a symbolic
way, it is not necessary to drill
holes thru the stem and the bowl.

16" to 20"

Section of
Stem.

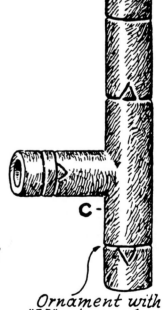

C-

Ornament with
"V" cuts made
with knife.

D- The stem is made of softwood & decorated
with black & red water color & shellaced
Feathers, fur, buckskin and red flannel are
used to ornament the stem. These may be
fastened on with glue or tied with thread

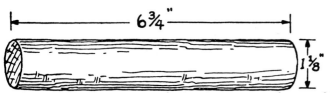

A – *Round pieces of Maple or Birch. Whittle smooth & sandpaper.*

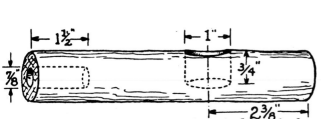

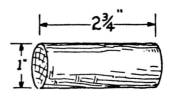

B – *Bore holes as indicated and glue together*

To put a realistic finish on the bowl which looks like real pipestone, take cream or buff colored flat wall paint and add red lead and a little lamp black to get a brick red color. Do not thin it. Put a stick into the stem hole to hold it, and apply the paint with a finger. When ornaments fill up with paint, scrape them out with a pointed stick. A second coat may be applied if the first does not look smooth enough. Run a hot iron around inside of bowl to give it a used look.

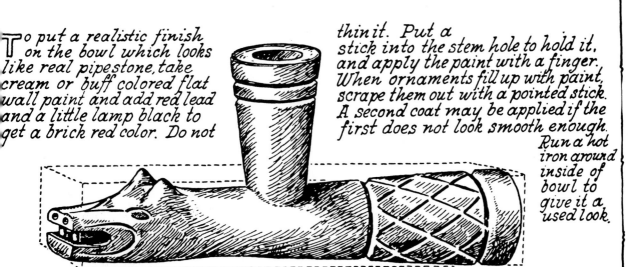

This pipe bowl is 6" long and 3" high, and was cut from a piece of wood 1⅛" square. The teeth are glued in place after the mouth is carved out.

CEREMONIAL INDIAN BOW AND ARROWS

Ceremonial bows and arrows are used only on special occasions, and the Indians like to use eagle wing feathers for decorating and fletching them. When these are unobtainable, hawk, owl, or the wing feathers of the wild goose are used. For our purpose, any feather will do. The fluffs mentioned are small feathers from the breasts of birds (see Figure 4). One is tied at the forward end of each arrow vane. Indians admired colored cloth, especially "turkey" red. Cloth of this color can be used for the wrappings on the bow. It may be either sewed or glued on.

While making this Indian ceremonial archery gear, do it as it was done by the Indians. The bow and arrows will then seem all the more real when they are hung on the wall or used for a dance or ceremony. Get some sinew from a butcher and use it instead of twine or string. The glue, too, might be put on with glue sticks like those made by the Indians. Take a small stick about ³⁄₁₆ inch square, and 5 inches long. Dip it in glue and let it dry repeatedly until a good lump of glue has been formed on its end (see Figure 5). This, when moistened and rubbed on the object to be glued, will work as nicely as a bottle of glue and a brush, and besides, it does not take up a lot of room.

The wrapping shown on the bow in the sketch is of fringed buckskin dyed yellow. This also is fastened on with glue.

Fig. 4

Fluff

Make these ceremonial bows weak rather than strong. There is then less danger of hurting anyone during a pageant or dance. To make double sure of avoiding an accident, the arrows may be strung onto the bow's string as shown in Figure 6.

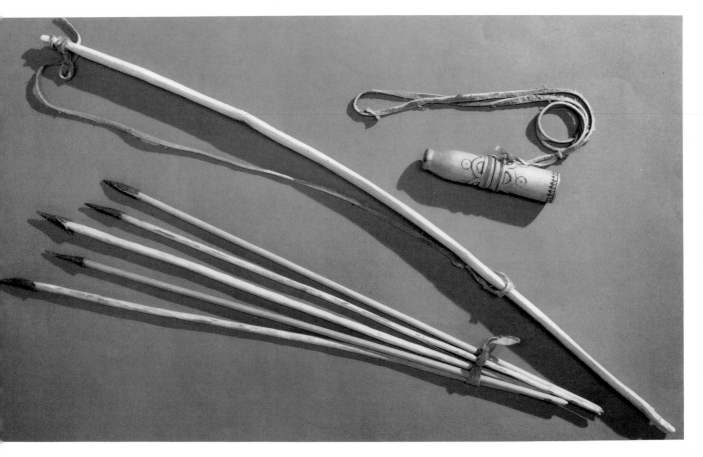

Bow and arrow; Kickapoo, Mexico. Photograph courtesy of Milwaukee Public Museum.

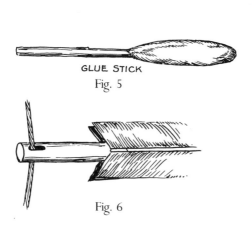

GLUE STICK
Fig. 5

Fig. 6

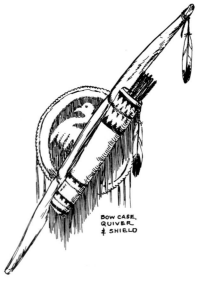

BOW CASE, QUIVER & SHIELD

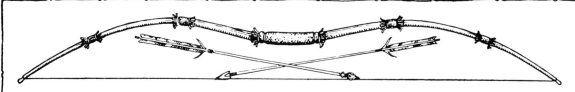

CEREMONIAL
INDIAN BOW AND ARROWS

BOWS The bow and arrows shown on this plate are for ceremonial and decorative purposes only, altho they are fashioned after the Indian tackle

In the modern bow, the handle or grip is set 2 inches off center while in this bow the handle is centered. Likewise with the arrows, the feathers are from 5 to 7 inches long whereas in modern arrows, the feathers are from

2 to 2½ inches long. While this bow will shoot the arrows with a fair degree of accuracy, it is not intended for that purpose. Both bow and arrows are for show only and as such can be made very attractive. Modern archery tackle is as much out of place in an Indian pageant or ceremony as an Indian dressed in a swallow tail coat and a silk hat.

1⅛" to 1¼"
¾"
Lay out on side of stave to used for back — 4" — 6" — 6" — 6" — 4"

Hickory or ash was used mostly by the Indians and is specified here because it is easy to obtain. The stave should be 48" long, 1½" wide and ½" thick. Mark as shown and cut out.

³⁄₈" Cut taper from belly of bow — The back of a bow is outside — the belly is the inner side, nearest the string

With a spokeshave trim down as smoothly as possible and taper the ends as shown above.
Carefully round off all edges with spokeshave or scraper or with a piece of glass.

Cut nocks with jackknife and finish with a round file or sandpaper.

Cut a form from a piece of 2"×4" and shape it as shown — Steam the middle section of the bow for about an hour and bend over the form.

2" 4" 15"

Use rope or clamps to fasten the bow to the form and let it dry for about 24 hours. Green wood need not be steamed but it should be left on the form for a week.

Instead of using seasoned wood, the Indian fashioned his bow of green wood, bent it to shape, rubbed it with grease & then let it season

When bow has dried for a week, string it to see if it bends evenly. If it does not, scrape down the stiff parts.

154

When the bow bends evenly, sandpaper it carefully, decorate with watercolor paint as shown above and give it several coats of linseed oil. When dry add the wrappings, which may be of buckskin or red cloth, glued and tied. Red, black & blue are suitable colors for painting which should be put on back of the bow.

Indians made their bowstrings of twisted sinew, but for our purpose a twisted cord about ⅜₂ thick will do. Tie the ends at the nocks and leave the bow strung. Bows of this kind do not look picturesque when unstrung.

ARROWS

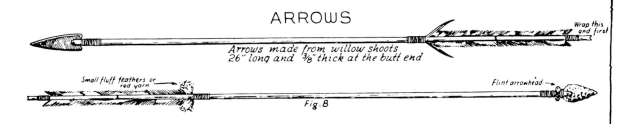

Arrows made from willow shoots
26" long and ⅜" thick at the butt end

Wrap this end first

Small fluff feathers or red yarn

Flint arrowhead →

Fig. 8

As a rule, modern arrows are made of birch or Port Orford cedar dowels. Indians used shoots of willow, dogwood, alder or any other straight shoots. Cut them about 28" long, peel them & tie them in a tight bundle, being careful that they are all straight. Let them dry for a week or two. Cut them about 24 or 26 inches long and carefully trim away any irregularities. This can be done with a small sharp plane. Fig. 1.

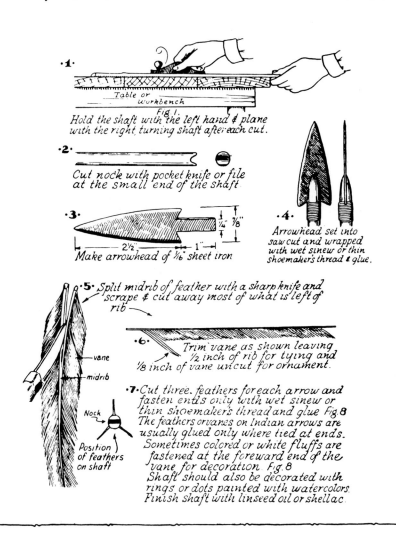

·1·
Table or Workbench
Fig. 1.
Hold the shaft with the left hand & plane with the right, turning shaft after each cut.

·2·
Cut nock with pocket knife or file at the small end of the shaft.

·3·
¼" ⅛"
2½" 1"
Make arrowhead of ¹⁄₁₆ sheet iron

·4·
Arrowhead set into saw cut and wrapped with wet sinew or thin shoemaker's thread & glue.

·5· Split midrib of feather with a sharp knife and scrape & cut away most of what is left of rib

·6· Trim vane as shown leaving ½ inch of rib for tying and ⅛ inch of vane uncut for ornament.

vane
midrib
Nock
Position of feathers on shaft

·7· Cut three feathers for each arrow and fasten ends only with wet sinew or thin shoemaker's thread and glue Fig. 8 The feathers or vanes on Indian arrows are usually glued only where tied at ends. Sometimes colored or white fluffs are fastened at the forward end of the vane for decoration Fig. 8 Shaft should also be decorated with rings or dots painted with watercolors. Finish shaft with linseed oil or shellac.

KACHINA DOLLS

These funny little dolls are made by the Hopi Indians shortly before the final Kachina, or religious ceremony. The final Kachina is called the "nimon," or homecoming Kachina, and comes about a month before the Hopi snake dance each year. Kachina dolls are representations of some of the Hopi gods. The men busy themselves in the kiva, or underground ceremonial house, preparing their costumes, and making kachinas (Hopi Tihus dolls) for the girls, and small red bows and arrows for the boys. No children are allowed in the kiva.

During the afternoon of the nimon, the kachina dolls are given to the little girls. The dolls may be the image of any one of the many Kachina spirits which are endowed with supernatural powers, and are usually clan ancestors.

Kachina dolls serve two purposes: They are an object lesson in religion for the children, and they are also attractive dolls. The little Indian girls carry them around in miniature cradles just as all children do. The kachinas are usually made of branches or small trees of some soft wood, but as the green wood takes some time to season, it is much more convenient to make them of one of the soft woods such as white pine, sugar pine, spruce, cedar, bass, or poplar which are very easy to whittle and easily obtainable at any lumberyard.

Kachina doll; Hopi. Photograph courtesy of Milwaukee Public Museum.

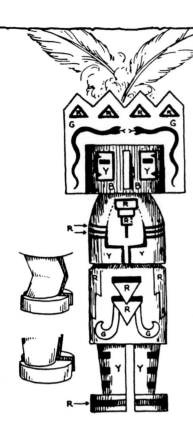

THE HOPIS
MAKE SOME
OF THEIR
DOLLS A
FOOT HIGH
BY TWO
TO THREE
INCHES IN
DIAMETER

ONE TO ONE AND ONE HALF
INCHES IN DIAMETER
IS ABOUT THE
EASIEST
SIZE TO
MAKE

DESIGNED
& DRAWN BY
W. BEN. HUNT,
HALES
CORNERS,
WIS.
1935

HOPI TIHUS DOLLS

TO FINISH-USE WATER
COLOR IF THE DOLLS ARE
NOT TO BE HANDLED MUCH
OTHERWISE USE EITHER
ENAMEL OR LACQUER.

COVER ENTIRE DOLL
WITH WHITE-WHEN
THAT IS DRY, PROCEED
WITH OTHER COLORS
AS SHOWN OR USE
YOUR OWN COLOR
SCHEME & DESIGNS

WHERE NO
COLOR IS
INDICATED
LEAVE WHITE

BLACK IS
SHOWN ON
DRAWINGS

R-RED
B-BLUE
Y-YELLOW
G-GREEN
O-ORANGE

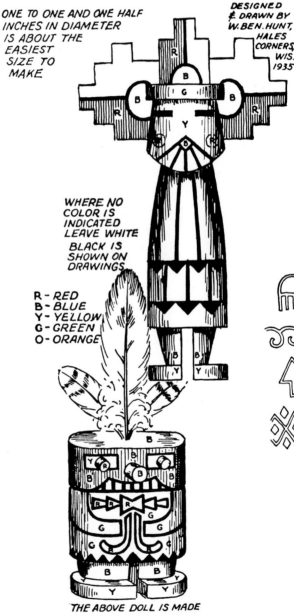

THE ABOVE DOLL IS MADE
FROM AN INCH BOARD.

FEATHERS AND
BITS OF FUR ARE
USUALLY USED
AS PART OF THE
HEAD ORNAMENT.

USE PINE, BASS
POPLAR, CEDAR
OR WILLOW.

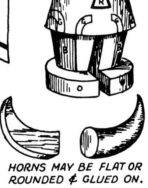

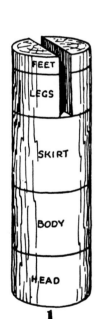

FEET

LEGS

SKIRT

BODY

HEAD

1

SLOT MAY BE CUT
OUT WITH COPING
SAW TO SAVE TIME.

MARK SEPARATIONS
WITH PENCIL.

USE A VERY
SHARP KNIFE.

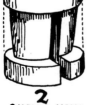

2

SHOWS HOW
FEET AND LEGS
ARE WHITTLED

3

NEXT CUT OUT
SKIRT—THEN
CUT AWAY AT
NECK AS SHOWN

HORNS MAY BE FLAT OR
ROUNDED & GLUED ON.

NOSES
ARE GLUED INTO
NOTCHES

4 AND
SET
NOSE
AND
HEAD
ORNA-
MENT
IN WITH
GLUE

3A
CUT ARMS NEXT

HEAD ORNAMENTS
ARE GLUED INTO SLOTS.

EYES ARE EITHER
CUT IN OR JUST
PAINTED ON.

SHIELDS

The woodland Indian used trees and rocks for shields, but the Plains Indian had no such protection. Therefore, he made himself a shield of heavy rawhide. It was more than just protection against arrows and bullets, it was his "medicine," for the Indian believed that it would protect him from all harm, and he made it so that the mere sight of it would strike terror into the hearts of his enemies. It was one of his most prized possessions and hung in the place of honor in his tepee, or in nice weather, he hung it up in front of the tepee. When not in battle, it was protected by a soft buckskin cover. After the coming of high-powered rifles, many of the Indians still carried a ceremonial, or medicine, shield made of thin rawhide or buckskin drawn taut over a hoop as shown in the plate.

Sometimes a loop large enough to go over the head and one shoulder was fastened to the shield. This enabled the warrior to carry it on his back in the same manner that a quiver is carried. Indians usually held their shields with two loops of buckskin, but the bent sticks illustrated on pages 162 and 163 make it easier to handle the shield for dance purposes.

When you make a cowhide shield, be sure to let the hide dry thoroughly before putting on any decorations. The inside edge of the shield may be stiffened by fastening it to a ½ inch round hoop every few inches with buckskin or thin rawhide thongs.

Hide shield with visionary designs (including celestial phenomena and zoomorphic spirits) used in the sun dance; Shoshone. Photograph courtesy of Milwaukee Public Museum.

PLAINS INDIAN SHIELDS

In the days before high-powered rifles, the war shield was the Plains Indian's most prized possession. Being rather small, from 16 to 20 inches in diameter, it could be easily handled, even while using a bow and arrows. A good shield would stop an arrow and ward off bullets from the old muzzle loading rifles. The best shields were made from rawhide from a buffalo's hump. Later they were made from raw cowhide. For ceremonial purposes they may be made from canvas, chamois skin, buckskin or even paper or "beaver-board".

AN EASY METHOD OF MAKING A CEREMONIAL SHIELD
OF BUCKSKIN, CHAMOIS OR CANVAS

If canvas is used give it a coat of cream colored flat wall paint before decorating.

·1· Make hoop of a 6 ft. green sapling. Peel it and trim it down to about ½ inch. Bend to shape while still green & tie with cord, buckskin or rawhide as shown.
To make a neat job, the overlaping ends should be tapered for about 10 inches.

·2· Material should be cut about 2 inches larger than hoop.

·3· Two bent sticks tied to hoop as shown, form arm loop and hand grip. (Note drawing on opposite plate.)

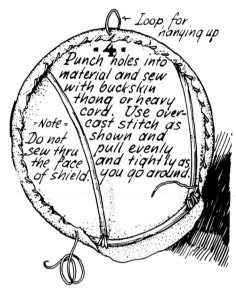

← *Loop for hanging up*

·4· Punch holes into material and sew with buckskin thong or heavy cord. Use overcast stitch as shown and pull evenly and tightly as you go around.

=Note= Do not sew thru the face of shield.

·5· For decorations see opposite plate.

A round piece of "beaver-board" or other building board can also be used. The sticks are tied to the back of the shield with thongs or heavy cord going thru the board and around the sticks. These sticks should be bowed so as to fit the arm & hand comfortably.

To MAKE A GOOD RAWHIDE SHIELD get a piece of raw cowhide. If hair is still on, scrape it off. **·1·** Cut to size wanted. **·2·** If dry, soak it in water until pliable. **·3·** Make a low mound of dry sand, and cover it with a piece of cloth. **·4·** Place wet rawhide over the cloth-covered mound, (Fig. I.) place another cloth over the rawhide and cover with more dry sand. It won't take long for it to dry on a nice hot day, but be sure it is dry before removing. It may have to be pounded some to shape it properly. **·5·** When thoroughly dry, fasten sticks to concave or hollow side as shown for "beaver board" shield. **·6·** The painting on the shield can be done with poster water colors. Sometimes a little glue has to be added but usually that is not required. **·7·** When water color has dried, a coat or two of furniture wax, or a coat of white shellac should be applied to both sides, to keep moisture out of the rawhide, and at the same time to tone down the water color, taking away that commercial appearance.

RAWHIDE
CLOTH
SAND   SAND

Fig. 1.

HOW SOME SHIELDS WERE DECORATED

How the shield is held in battle

On this page are shown 3 attractive shields such as were made and used by the Plains Indians. Painted and decorated in this manner, any 16 inch disk, if only of paper stretched over a narrow hoop, will make a striking decoration.

Of course, if the shield is made of raw-hide it will be more realistic, but no more attractive.

If oil paint is used, try and get "flat" paint. Glossy paint spoils the effect.

Owl feathers and fluffs.

RED

RED

WHITE

BLACK
RED

BLACK

Red
Blue
White

Bear claws tied on with thongs.

Eagle feathers and a piece of red flannel.

Owl feathers

The Indian's shield was his "medicine" It protected him from harm and gave him wonderful powers. It was supposed to terrify his enemies and had mysterious qualities which only the owner knew about. The painting and the objects tied to the shield, all had their special meanings and qualities which were in turn imparted to the owner of the shield.

The red flannel on the two lower shields goes around the back as far as it does in front, and is fastened by tying as shown

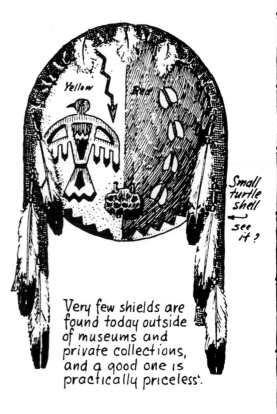

Punch holes for tying.

Yellow

Small turtle shell ← see it?

Very few shields are found today outside of museums and private collections, and a good one is practically priceless.

Reddish brown

Blue   Blue

Red →

Red?

White eagle feathers were always used when on hand, still other feathers were valued for their significance. The owl feather meant sight at night. The crow has wonderful sight in the daytime. So don't be afraid to use your imagination, and don't be afraid to make changes in the designs shown here

INDIAN WAR CLUBS

Before the coming of the white man, the Indians used stone and wood for their war clubs. On the opposite page three types of war clubs are shown. Several shapes of stone ax heads and war club heads also are shown. They may be duplicated in wood, and after they have been nicely whittled, a coat of gray flat wall paint followed by a sprinkling of sand will give them a realistic appearance.

Iron and steel tomahawks were usually made for the Indians by white blacksmiths, who did quite a business trading the tomahawks for animal skins. This type of tomahawk also may be imitated in wood and painted to look like steel or iron. Because of the thin edge, they should be made of hard wood.

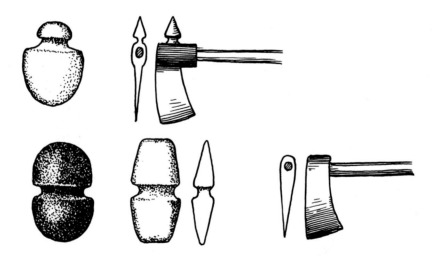

Man in costume, No Flesh; Oglala Sioux, South Dakota. Photograph courtesy of Smithsonian Institution, National Museum of the American Indian.

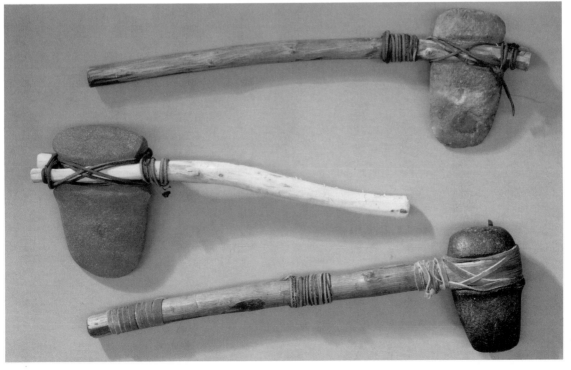

Reconstruction of axes used by prehistoric Indians in the Midwest. Photograph courtesy of Milwaukee Public Museum.

INDIAN WAR CLUBS

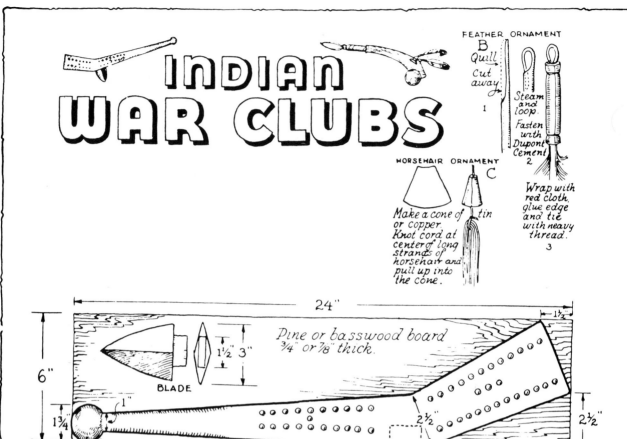

FEATHER ORNAMENT

B Quill
Cut away
1

Steam and loop.
Fasten with Dupont Cement
2

Wrap with red cloth, glue edge and tie with heavy thread.
3

HORSEHAIR ORNAMENT

C

Make a cone of tin or copper. Knot cord at center of long strands of horsehair and pull up into the cone.

24"

1½"

Pine or basswood board ¾" or ⅞" thick.

1½" 3"

BLADE

6"

1"

1¾"

2½"

2½"

17"

Round off at the grip or handle.
Decorate with round-headed brass upholstering tacks after the club is painted.

Paint the blade black and the rest of the club a dull brownish red. Originally the blade was of iron.

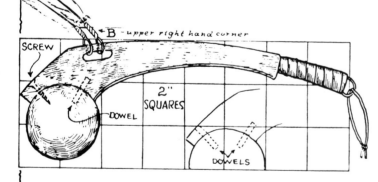

B — upper right hand corner

SCREW

2" SQUARES

DOWEL

DOWELS

Cut handle from a piece of 1" pine. Use an old croquet ball, about 3" or 3½" in diameter, for the knob. Fasten as shown, with a dowel set in glue and a 1½" screw, or with two dowels, the one at the end being driven in last. If a screw is used be sure to countersink it and cover it afterwards.

This war club may be painted with red and yellow paint. The handle should be rounded and covered with buckskin, wrapped spirally over a loop fastened with with small nails. Two or three feathers, as shown, complete the job.

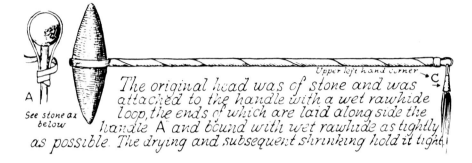

The original head was of stone and was attached to the handle with a wet rawhide loop, the ends of which are laid along side the handle A and bound with wet rawhide as tightly as possible. The drying and subsequent shrinking hold it tight.

Upper left hand corner C

A
See stone ax below

The head is 2 inches in diameter and 5 inches long and can be whittled out of any kind of wood. To fasten the handle, bore a hole the proper size (about ¾") thru the head, and wrap once around the head with buckskin and also the entire length of the handle. Put a loop at the end to fasten some suitable ornament. Paint the head a brownish gray color to represent stone.

INDIAN STONE AX

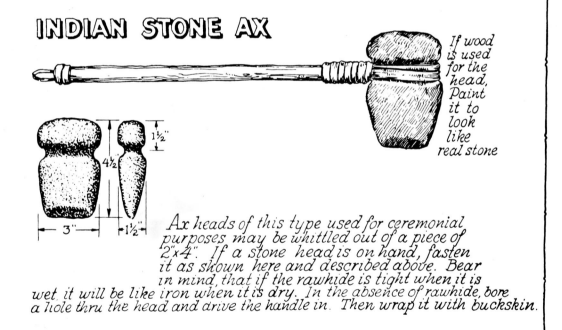

If wood is used for the head, Paint it to look like real stone

4½"
3"
1½"
1½"

Ax heads of this type used for ceremonial purposes may be whittled out of a piece of 2"x4". If a stone head is on hand, fasten it as shown here and described above. Bear in mind, that if the rawhide is tight when it is wet, it will be like iron when it is dry. In the absence of rawhide, bore a hole thru the head and drive the handle in. Then wrap it with buckskin.

A CHIPPEWA FISH SPEAR

1½" to 2"

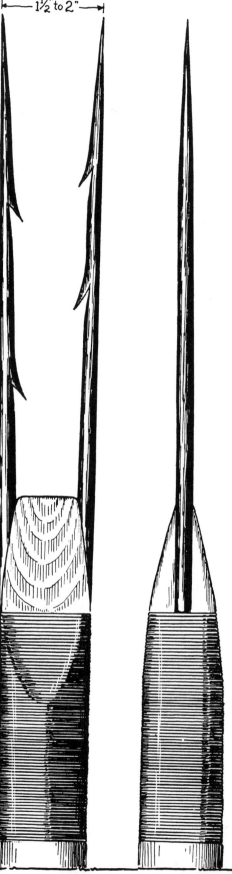

This is the type of spear used by some of the Indians of Northern Wisconsin. The prongs are made of wrought iron or soft steel Then if you strike a stone and bend them, they can easily be hammered straight again. Spearing suckers, carp, garfish, etc., is a lot of fun, but it is unlawful in some localities. So be sure to consult your game laws.

1. Get a pole of light wood about 1¼ to 1½ inches at the butt end and about 8 or 10 feet long. Trim it carefully and straighten it while green.

2. You will need two pieces of ¼ in. rod about 12 to 15 in. long. File a long point at one end and a short point at the other end of each rod. One rod should be one inch longer than the other

3. Bend short points over as shown at "A." Cut barbs with sharp cold chisel. This can be done cold if necessary. Hold rod in vise as shown.

A ↕ ⅜"

If a forge or fire is handy, heat the iron for bending and cutting barbs

4. Cut butt end of pole to chisel edge and cut grooves for barbs

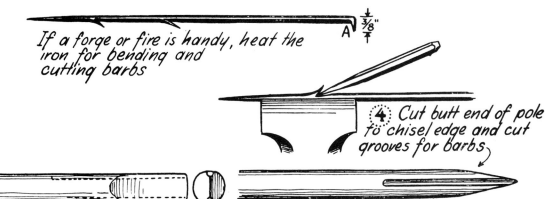

5. Drive short points into shaft. When set, prongs should taper slightly outward

6. Wrap with trolling line and shellack, or with wire. If pole is cut down to allow for wrapping it will tend to give your spear more stream line.

FROG SPEARS

There are times when one runs into a mess of nice frogs and has no way of catching them. That's when these spears will come in handy. All you need is a few sticks, some cord and a pocket knife. If you can scare up a piece of old fish pole (bamboo) for the prongs, so much the better.

1 First of all you will need a pole, about 1 inch at the butt and from 6 to 10 feet long. Peel it and trim it fairly smooth.

2 Then get some tough hard wood for the prongs. Bamboo, hickory, ironwood or ash are very good. Whittle them as shown below. This is the easy way.

Length and thickness depend on the size of the frogs you are going after. 6 inch prongs would be average size.

3 Or you can make the prongs the Eskimo way, with the barbs fitted and tied to the prongs with

thin fish line or fine copper wire.

④ Now whittle the butt end of   the pole to fit the prongs. This is done almost like the one for the fish spear, except that

the prongs should have quite a bit more spread.

⑤ Fasten prongs to pole with copper wire or fish line, or in a pinch they can be tied with basswood bark.

The prongs should be springy enough to open up when hitting a frog, and then sort of pinching it to hold it.

2

This type of spear may be used for small fish as well as frogs. The prongs should also have a certain amount of spring.

The center prong may be added to help hold fish or frogs. It is just a piece of pointed hardwood set into pole.

173

Harpooning; Nootka. Photograph courtesy of Smithsonian Institution,
National Museum of the American Indian.

LACROSSE STICKS

Have you ever tried catching and throwing with Indian lacrosse sticks? The loop is just large enough to hold the ball loosely and, as shown, takes only one-half of the ball. The game of lacrosse is usually played with a soft ball similar to our soft baseball, but wooden balls of cedar are also used at times. Make a pair of these sticks and try them out. It's fun making them, as the soft green wood is quite pliable and easy to whittle. The stick, made of 1 inch sapling, can be whittled and shaped in less than an hour. Then, in a day or two of warm dry weather, it can be permanently tied.

The rules of the game vary. Usually, it is played with five men on a team. Similar to basketball, the ball is tossed up in the center of the field, and the goal posts are set 5 to 6 feet apart at each end of the field. The ball must not be touched with the hands, and players are penalized for using their hands on the ball. The ball must be thrown so that it passes between the goal posts to score. It is a game which requires great skill and endurance.

Lacrosse stick; Kickapoo. Photograph courtesy of Milwaukee Public Museum.

LACROSSE STICKS

The game of lacrosse was played by the Indians before the white man came to this country. Whereas the old Indian game was rather rough and played with many players, today it is simplified and has become a real game of skill. Try making a pair of these ball sticks, as they were called, and then try playing "catch" with them. It will be found rather tricky at first but once mastered it is a lot of fun.

Two types of sticks are shown, but the method of making them is practically the same. Indians usually make them of green ash or hickory, but almost any green wood can be used. The overall size is usually about 3 feet long. In a game they should all be the same length.

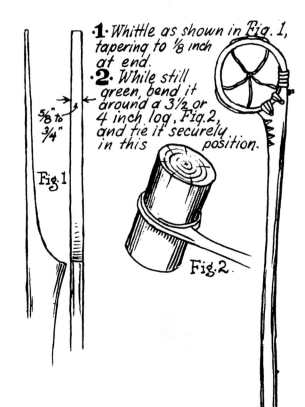

1. Whittle as shown in Fig. 1, tapering to 1/8 inch at end.

2. While still green, bend it around a 3½ or 4 inch log, Fig.2, and tie it securely in this position.

5/8" to 3/4"

Fig.1

Fig.2

Tie it in any way you see fit. The main thing is to hold it in position until dry. This may take a few days if kept in a dry place.

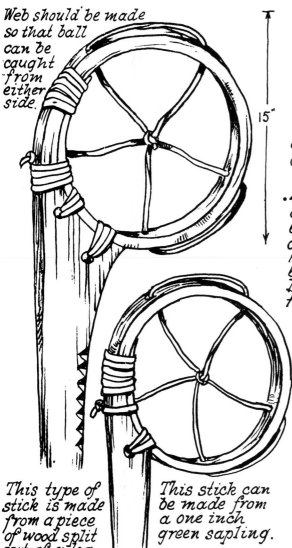

Web should be made
so that ball
can be
caught
from
either
side.

15"

This type of
stick is made
from a piece
of wood split
out of a log.

This stick can
be made from
a one inch
green sapling.

·3· Then bore holes as
shown at left and bind
the end down firmly.
Indians used buckskin or
rawhide for this, but a
good grade of braided
cord will do.

·4· Drill 5 holes as shown
at left and fasten webbing of
buckskin, leather shoe string,
or heavy cord. When ball is
in pocket, half of it should
be hidden as shown below.
Ball should fit "nicely", not too
tight and not too loose.

·5· Shape the handle to suit your
personal grip. A little carving is
sometimes done as shown.

·6· Lacrosse balls are
about 3 inches in
diameter and are
made like a soft
baseball and sometimes
they are whittled out of
some light wood.

THROWING STICK

The Southwest Indians of today find a .22 caliber rifle or a slingshot better for getting rabbits than the throwing stick, although some of these sticks are still used at times. The author made one from a crooked branch of a red oak tree, with nothing more than a small hand ax to do the whittling.

THROWING ARROWS

The game of throwing arrows is not as strenuous as lacrosse, but just as much skill is required. On the Crow Indian Reservation, the game is played every Sunday when the weather permits. Some of the arrows have elaborate points, forged and filed to shape; some are wrapped with rawhide and some with wire; but the feathers are always tied with sinew. The smaller marker arrow is not as fancy as the throwing arrow, because there sometimes are a great many players and the marker gets the worst of it, as every target does.

Grizzly bears attacking Indians on horseback, George Catlin, 1832–33.
Photograph courtesy of Smithsonian Institution, National Museum of
the American Indian.

CROW THROWING ARROWS

The Crow Indian's game of throwing arrows is somewhat similar to our game of pitching horseshoes, but instead of fixed stakes to throw at, a somewhat lighter arrow is first thrown by one of the players as far as possible. The players then throw their arrows at this marker arrow and of course the closest arrow wins. The winner then throws the marker arrow as far as he can and they all try again, etc. Each player has two throwing arrows and of course someone must have a marker.

Three long feathers are tied on the small end as shown above and at left, spaced equidistant as for regular archery arrows. No glue is necessary, but feathers should be quite tight and wrappings should be shellacked or varnished.

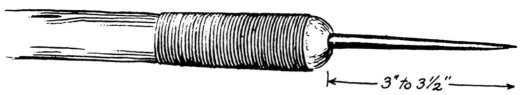

← 3" to 3½" →

An iron or steel point is then set into a hole drilled into the large end of the shaft, and shaft is bound tightly with rawhide or soft wire to prevent splitting.

Throwing an Arrow.

HOPI
THROWING STICK

These sticks are used by Hopi and other Southwest Indians for killing small game and are sometimes called rabbit sticks. They are made from a crooked branch, whittled flat as shown and sometimes decorated.

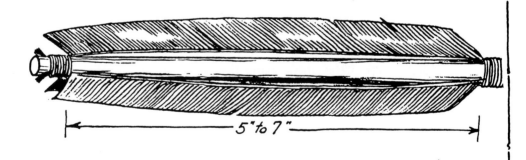

HANDLE

RED

SECTION

4¾"

SECTION

BLACK

8"

2"

RED

13"

No two sticks are alike. They are all bent like this one but some much thinner and lighter.
These are not boomerangs. Some sticks are carved, others painted, most of them are plain.

Wrapping at balancing point.

Select two straight saplings measuring ¾ to 1 inch at the thick end and about 4 feet long. Wild cherry is best but is not always available. Trim them down smoothly from ¾" thick at the point to ⅜" at the feathered end, straighten, and let them dry for a week or so.

5" to 7"

INDIAN HOOP GAME

Among some tribes, the hoop game is as popular as lacrosse and throwing arrows. The hoop opposite is most easily made of green willow, ash, hickory, hazel or elm. But any green wood that will stand bending will do. The hoop does not require as much strength as lacrosse sticks.

Indians usually made the webbing out of rawhide. In some cases a simple four-part hoop was used; in other cases an elaborate web was woven similar to snowshoe webbing. The one shown is webbed with ⅛-inch twisted cord and is quite a simple pattern. The lance or stick used for throwing can be made of any straight stick as shown. The game is simple, but it requires a lot of skill to get a good score quickly.

The hoop is rolled on a smooth flat plot of ground and the player throws his lance at it, trying to hit the center opening if possible. The count varies with the type of webbing used. With this hoop, the count could be 5 for the outer openings, 10 for the next row, 25 for the next row which are quite a bit smaller and 100 for the center opening.

Each player, of course, gets one throw at the hoop in turn, and the one getting the most points in 10, 15, or 20 throws is the winner.

Rules can be varied. If the lance goes entirely through any of the openings, it does not count at all, as there is no proof as to which opening it went through. The lance may also be divided into four painted sections. Then additional points could be added according to which section is in the webbing when the hoop is stopped, the first section counting more than the end section.

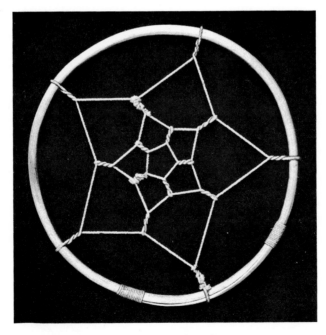

Hoop webbed with a heavy twisted cord.

INDIAN HOOP GAME

This is a simple game which requires very little equipment but calls for a lot of skill to get a high score.

Make hoop of green willow, ash, hickory or any other wood that will take a bend.

Before bending, trim it down to an even thickness of about ½ inch.

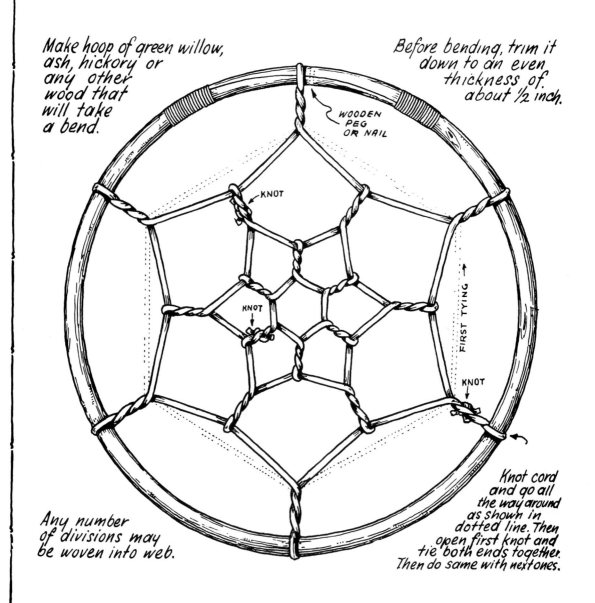

WOODEN PEG OR NAIL

KNOT

KNOT

FIRST TYING →

KNOT

Any number of divisions may be woven into web.

Knot cord and go all the way around as shown in dotted line. Then open first knot and tie both ends together. Then do same with next ones.

Lance may be of any length from 3 to 6 ft, or more & should taper as shown.

For a 12 or 14 inch hoop, cut a straight switch about 6 feet long. After trimming it down to an even thickness, bend it slowly around a stump or tree, or a water pail, or any cylinder of the proper diameter. Tie the ends and let it dry for a day or so. Then mark where ends should be cut off, allowing about 8 or 10 inches of overlap. Untie it, take it off of form, and taper the ends as shown above. Now wrap the ends and drive a nail or a peg through to keep it from slipping.
For webbing, use a leather thong or heavy cord. (about ⅛" thick) The webbing shown above is quite simple, each round being a separate cord.

BOX TRAPS

Probably, the first box traps were made from a hollow log, since such logs make an ideal trap and fit into the surroundings. Box traps are most efficient right after a heavy snowstorm when rabbits and small game have a hard time finding food. Do not close up the lower end with a solid board, because animals like to see where they are going.

If you have a lot of small trees and shrubs it is a good idea to set one or two of these traps beneath them during the winter, when rabbits do the most damage. Train your dog to stay away from these traps. Many small dogs have spent hours in a box trap while their masters scoured the countryside looking for them.

The effectiveness of the box trap is demonstrated by the experience of two Indian boys who wanted a chipmunk for a pet. They set a box trap to catch one, but before they finally succeeded, they had caught and liberated two cats, one dog, one skunk, and three robins.

Man in costume; Oglala Sioux, South Dakota. Photograph courtesy of Smithsonian Institution, National Museum of the American Indian.

HOW TO MAKE GOOD OLD RELIABLE
BOX TRAPS

Box traps are used when one wishes to catch small animals alive. Another advantage in using them is, that should a useful or harmless animal be caught, it can be released unharmed. Box traps can be used to catch rabbits, chipmunks, rats, stray cats, skunks, etc. They should be made of old weathered boards if possible.

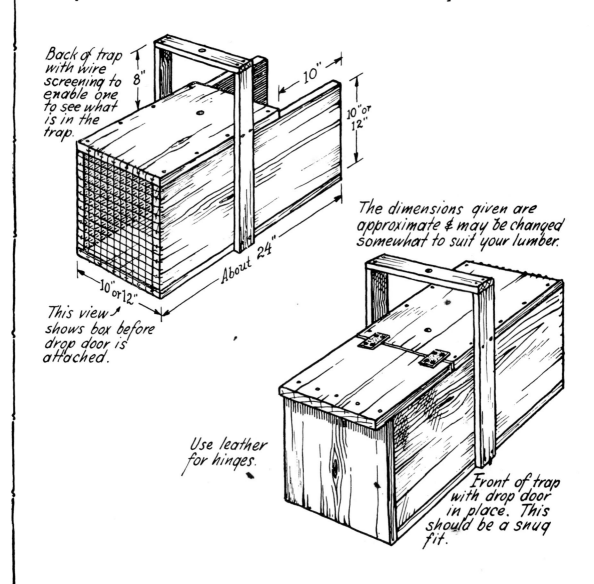

Back of trap with wire screening to enable one to see what is in the trap.

8"

10"

10" or 12"

The dimensions given are approximate & may be changed somewhat to suit your lumber.

About 24"

10" or 12"

This view shows box before drop door is attached.

Use leather for hinges.

Front of trap with drop door in place. This should be a snug fit.

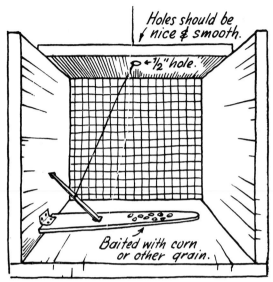

Holes should be nice & smooth.

←½" hole.

Baited with corn or other grain.

How the trigger arrangement looks when set, showing flat trigger. When apples or carrots are used for bait, they can be tied to the trigger or one like this can be made.

Notch   Bait

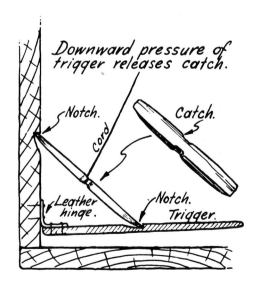

Downward pressure of trigger releases catch.

Notch.

Catch.

Cord

Leather hinge.

Notch. Trigger.

Trigger arrangement. If weight of drop-door does not hold up the trigger, tie a flat stone to top of door or undercut the notches more.

A block of wood may be nailed inside of door to strengthen it

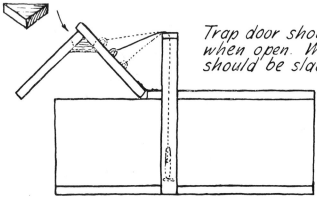

Trap door should be in this position when open. When closed, the cord should be slack. Therefore you may have to experiment a little to find out just where to place the screw eye (or staple) in the top of the door.

A two door trap which permits animals to enter from either end is sometimes better than a one door trap. It requires a little more time to build, but may be worth it. Both cords are fastened to the catch, for of course, both doors must close at the same instant.

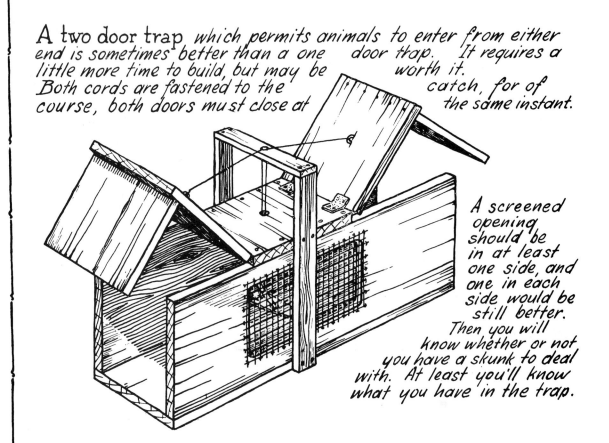

A screened opening should be in at least one side, and one in each side would be still better. Then you will know whether or not you have a skunk to deal with. At least you'll know what you have in the trap.

A BACKWOODS BOX TRAP AND A FIGURE 4 TRIGGER

In a pinch, this trap can be made with nothing more than a pocket knife.

Make the box of one inch saplings, notched and nailed or tied together as shown.

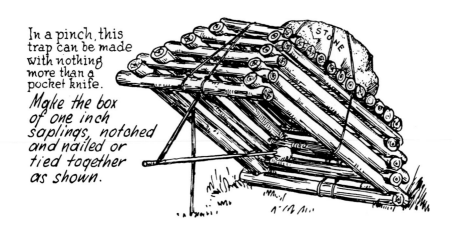

Down pressure on this stick holds trigger in place, and box up.
A slight jiggling of the baited end and the whole thing collapses and the box falls.

Bait end

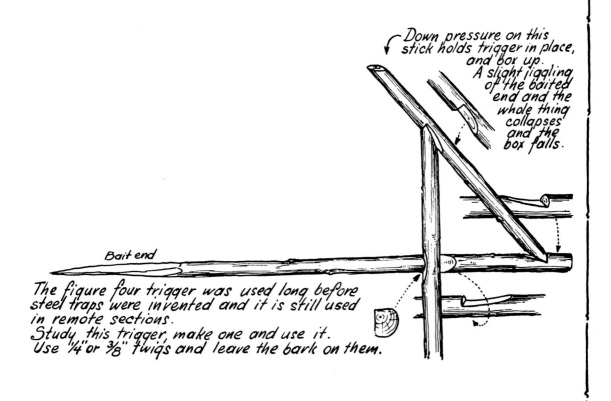

The figure four trigger was used long before steel traps were invented and it is still used in remote sections.
Study this trigger, make one and use it.
Use ¼" or ⅜" twigs and leave the bark on them.

INDIAN TOTEM POLES

A totem pole is a column of wood, usually cedar, carved with figures that have symbolic meaning. The poles show animals, fish, birds, and creatures from tales and legends. A family symbol, something like a coat-of-arms, is often carved onto the pole.

TOTEM POLE

Everyone loves to work on a totem pole. It is a job in which you can use a chisel and a mallet to your heart's content, and use your ingenuity as well. Carving a totem pole is fun, from trimming down the pole, to setting it up out of doors for all the world to see.

Two, or sometimes three people, can work on a pole at the same time. Assign a section to each worker and indicate these assignments on a sketch or on a miniature. Then let one person work at the top section, another at the middle section, and still another at the lower part. In this way, they will not interfere with one another's work. When the rough work is finished, they may be assigned to work on the next lower sections. And finally, those who are good at whittling should be set to trim and finish up details with pocketknives.

When putting on the colored paint, it is best to paint with only one color at a time, letting that dry before applying the next color. In this way, there will be less chance for smearing, or for colors to run together.

Totem pole; Kwakiutl, Albert Bay, British Columbia. Photograph
courtesy of Milwaukee Public Museum.

TOTEM POLE

Pole should be about 10" or 12" thick at butt end and from 10' to 14' long depending on where it is to be used and the material available.

If a bass or pine log is used, peel off bark & trim away any bumps or irregularities with a drawknife.

If an old telephone pole is used, cut away the gray or weathered outside layer with a drawknife. Large checks or cracks may be filled with strips of wood or putty after carving is completed.

Decide what symbols or designs you wish to use and lay out each section full size on wrapping paper or on a blackboard. A better plan is to whittle a small model first, using a piece of pine one inch in diameter.

Place the pole on horses or blocks about 2' from the ground and

block it with wedges to prevent it from rolling.

With a soft pencil or a piece of crayon draw a line around the pole to show where each section begins & ends.

Lay the pole with the smoothest side up, as totem poles are only carved on one side, and lay out the top section with crayon.

Socket firmer chisels, a wooden mallet and a camp knife are about all the tools necessary to do the carving.

Leave about 3' to go into ground

Now start carving. Outline the section to be cut out with a chisel using the same number of blows for each cut. Then by prying gently, the waste wood may be lifted out in layers. After the required depth has been reached the lowered surface should be smoothed down nicely & the raised edges should be rounded off.

Where large lettering is used, it may be cut out or the background may be cut away and the lettering left standing. Small lettering is best painted on.

These sketches were made from the pole before the colored paint was put on.

Wings & beaks are cut out of inch boards and are set into mortises about 2" deep. Nails driven at angles from both sides will hold them in place.

Pieces accidentally broken out may be given a coating of white lead and fastened back in place with thin finishing nails.

If two wish to work at the same time, lay out the top and middle sections, and each may work downward without interfering.

To finish, give the pole a priming coat of white paint and then paint the entire pole with colored paints to suit, thus giving it two coats overall.

Added ornamentations may be painted on, as for instance, eyes, teeth, feathers, etc.

For colors, use black, brown, red, blue, green and yellow with a little white here and there to form a contrast.

SNOW GOGGLES

These wooden goggles may seem rather primitive, but they are really better than smoked- or tinted-glass goggles as a protection against the sun. First, they fit more closely to the face, and so do not get caught in brush so easily. Secondly, the glare reflected from below does not bother the wearer, and thirdly, they do not get steamed up. You can also see well enough through them to use a gun or a camera.

If no thick wood is available, make the goggles in two parts and hinge them together over the nose. Use a piece of leather thong for the hinge.

Goggles like those shown can be made of ½-inch box lumber or any small pieces of wood. They can be folded up and put in a small pocket when they are not being worn.

The goggles shown below and in the plate were made with a sort of visor running across, which also acts as a reinforcing strip.

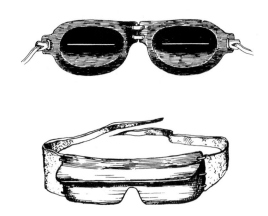

Killer whale on sun mask: wood and cloth; Kwakiutl. Photograph
courtesy of Milwaukee Public Museum.

SNOW GOGGLES

In extreme cases soot is also rubbed all around the eyes and on the lids.

These goggles do your squinting for you. They are used by Eskimos, Indians & trappers in the far north as a protection against snowblindness. The narrow slits and the blackened inner side keep out most of the intense glare of the sun on ice and snow and still enable the wearer to see well enough for all practical purposes.

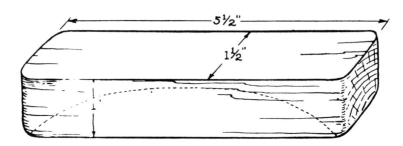

5½"

1½"

·1·
Any soft wood (or better still, walnut, of which the ones described are made) may be used. It should be straight grained. Round off the corners. Then with a piece of cardboard and shears make a template of the curve of the forehead at the line of the eyebrows.

·2·
Mark the line on the edge of the block and cut out as shown at right. Goggles should not fit too close or steam will form on the inside on cold days.

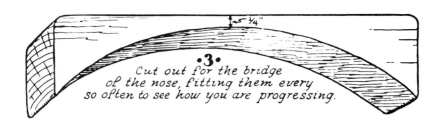

•3•
*Cut out for the bridge
of the nose, fitting them every
so often to see how you are progressing.*

•4•
*Clamp in vise and cut out the
depressions with a gouge or knife.
The depressions or hollows
should be from ⅜ to ½ inch
deep at the deepest point.*

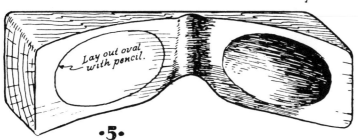

*Lay out oval
with pencil.*

•5•
*Then cut away the surplus wood
to about the shape shown here.
Care must be taken not to cut away
too much at first. The slits are then
cut out with the point of a knife and
a keyhole saw if one is handy.*

•6•
*Cutting the slits enables you to
see exactly how thick the wood is.
If too thick, it can easily be trimmed
down to about 1/16 of an inch at the
thinnest part which is right at
the slit.*

*Cut small slots at the ends for
buckskin thongs with which the
goggles are tied on.*

*Paint the inside and the edges of
the slits with a dull black paint.
The outer side may be painted, shellaked
or finished with a coat of linseed oil.*

Inner side of completed goggles.

ARCTIC HAND SLED

This is a picturesque sled, well adapted for winter hikes and overnight camping trips. It is not intended for coasting, but for hauling only. While it is used as a hand sled in the far north, it can be pulled by one or two dogs.

The runners are made of a hickory or ash sapling, about 1½ inches thick at the butt end. Peel the bark off and rip it through the center. Smooth the cut side with a spokeshave. Then put the two butt ends in a woodworker's vise, one above the other, and clamp tightly. Then slowly work them to the position shown. Green wood will bend easily if worked gradually. Tie a rope around the two runners, and stick a piece of wood under the ends to support them (see Figure 1). If the bending is done in a warm dry place, the wood will be permanently set in a week's time.

In a land where traveling for the greatest part of the year is over snow and ice, it is only natural that there are many kinds of sleds. The one described here may be made by anyone who has sufficient patience and is willing to stick on the job.

Sleds like the one shown sometimes have wood runners (Figure 2) fastened with walrus hide. The top boards are usually ⅜ inch thick and 2 or 3 inches wide; and, as lumber is scarce in Eskimo land, they are laid ½ to 1 inch apart.

The main thing in making a sled like this is to see that the rawhide fastenings are drawn up as tightly as possible, and that the ends of the lashings are secured. Don't let this type of sled stand out in the rain or dampness unless the rawhide has a good coat of oil or varnish.

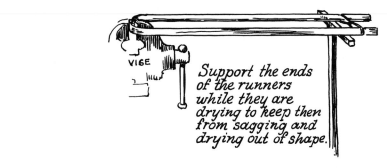

Fig. 1

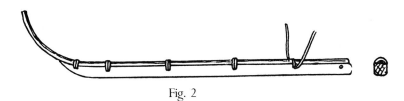

Fig. 2

ARCTIC HAND SLED

These sleds are used for hauling when no dogs are available or when a man pulls with one or two dogs. If a longer sled is wanted, simply add one or more sections. It is made entirely of wood and rawhide except for the shoes.
Green hickory & ash saplings were used for the one shown here. Runners are of 1¾" saplings split with a ripsaw, bows are of 1-inch saplings, bent while green.

This crosspiece is not needed if top boards are laid crosswise

Sled frame without top.

SHOES MADE OF BAND IRON OR SHEET IRON.

PARTS of SLED
① Runners......2
② Bows..........3
③ Uprights......6
④ Crosspieces....4
⑤ Side rails....2
⑥ Top rails......2
⑦ Pull bar......1
⑧ Shoes..........2
Top boards
(not shown)

Eskimo sleds are usually built of odds and ends washed up by the sea or obtained from whalers. The different parts are tied together with walrus-hide thongs. If nails or screws were used, the wood would split when the sled received rough usage, but by using walrus-hide or rawhide fastenings, the sled becomes quite flexible and therefore is less likely to be broken. It is also easier to repair while on the trail as thongs of hide are always carried along.

The sled shown above is 43 inches long, 16 inches wide and about 6 inches high. The top rails at the rear of the sled are about 15 inches from the bottom of the runners. Note the slight upturn of the side rails at the front end of sled.

Rawhide should be soaked in water for about 12 hours before using and should be pulled as tight as possible when used.

Saplings should be peeled.

vise

Side view

BENDING RUNNERS

vise →

Top view.
Bend slowly until correct shape is attained. Tie as shown and prop up the ends so they don't sag. Let dry for a week or two.

rope

Runners are about 52 inches long before bending

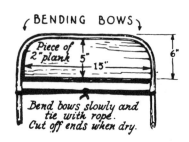

BENDING BOWS

Piece of 2" plank
5"
15"
6"

Bend bows slowly and tie with rope. Cut off ends when dry.

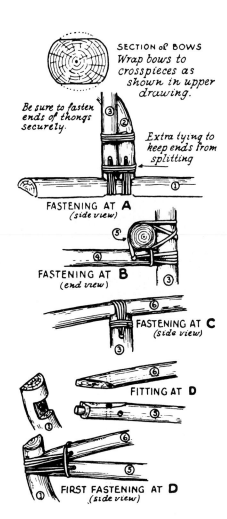

SECTION of BOWS

Wrap bows to crosspieces as shown in upper drawing.

Be sure to fasten ends of thongs securely.

Extra tying to keep ends from splitting

FASTENING AT **A**
(side view)

FASTENING AT **B**
(end view)

FASTENING AT **C**
(side view)

FITTING AT **D**

FIRST FASTENING AT **D**
(side view)

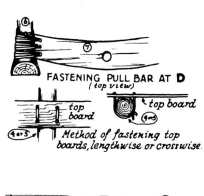

FASTENING PULL BAR AT **D**
(top view)

top board

top board

Method of fastening top boards, lengthwise or crosswise.

4"

2½"

PULL BAR

made of one-inch board to fit between side rails.

Below is shown how parts are set together with short mortise & tenons before tying with rawhide.

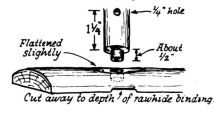

¼" hole

1¼"

Flattened slightly

About ½"

Cut away to depth of rawhide binding.

runner

shoe

SECTIONAL VIEW OF RUNNERS

The only metal used is the strap-iron shoes and the screws to fasten them. Screws should be countersunk.

The Eskimos use iron or even tin when they can get it, but otherwise their sleds are shod with whalebone or thick rawhide. Sometimes shoes are made of wood fastened to the runners with walrus-hide thongs

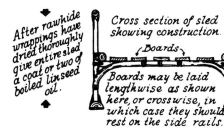

After rawhide wrappings have dried thoroughly give entire sled a coat or two of boiled linseed oil.

Cross section of sled showing construction.

Boards

Boards may be laid lengthwise as shown here, or crosswise, in which case they should rest on the side rails.

INDIAN SNOWSHOES OF WOOD

For a cross-country hike in winter, nothing compares with snowshoes, and it is easy to learn how to use them. The snowshoes shown are easy to make and with reasonable care will last a long time. The shape may be changed to suit the individual. They may be made in a few hours, and need only be oiled once in a while to keep them in good condition.

Wooden snowshoes will not take the rough usage that webbed ones will; but they are much more easily and quickly made.

Game wardens put on and take off their snowshoes a great many times during a day's work. For this reason, they use the type of harness shown in Figure 3, with a large rubber band cut from an old inner tube to keep the foot in place. The leather toe sleeve is fastened permanently to the snowshoe.

To put on snowshoes equipped with this type of harness, hook the rubber band over the back of the shoe, slip the toe of the shoe into the leather toe sleeve, and loop the rubber band under the toe, as shown. This keeps the shoe snug in the toe sleeve and the snowshoes can be quickly taken off when necessary. This harness works best when using heavy-soled shoes, as the pull of the rubber band would be uncomfortable when wearing moccasins or sneakers.

INNER TUBE RUBBER BAND

Boot is fastened thru holes in wooden snow-shoe or around thongs in webbed snow shoe.

Fig. 3

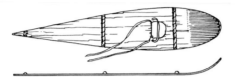

Snowshoe with slightly different design.

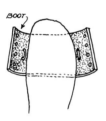

BOOT

Leather toe sleeve.

WOODEN SNOWSHOES

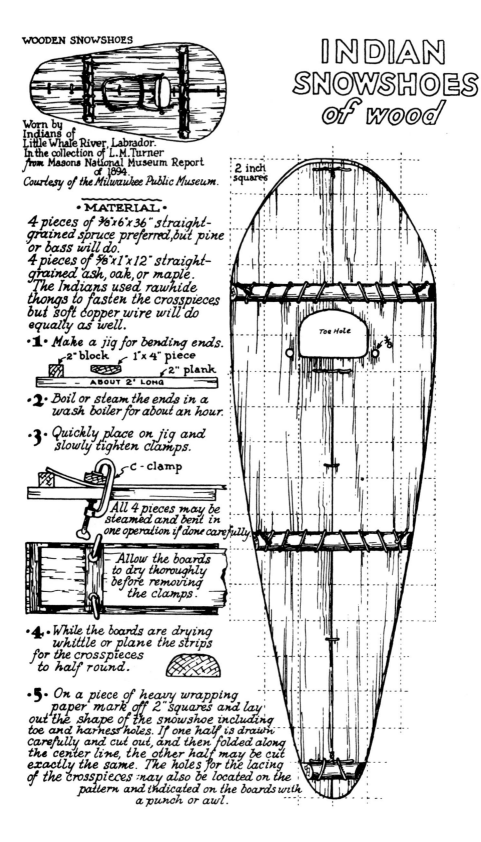

Worn by
Indians of
Little Whale River, Labrador.
In the collection of L.M.Turner
from Masons National Museum Report
of 1894.
Courtesy of the Milwaukee Public Museum.

INDIAN SNOWSHOES *of wood*

· MATERIAL ·

4 pieces of ⅜"x 6"x 36" straight-grained spruce preferred, but pine or bass will do.
4 pieces of ⅝"x 1"x 12" straight-grained ash, oak, or maple.
The Indians used rawhide thongs to fasten the crosspieces but soft copper wire will do equally as well.

·1· Make a jig for bending ends.

2" block   1"x 4" piece
2" plank
— ABOUT 2' LONG —

·2· Boil or steam the ends in a wash boiler for about an hour.

·3· Quickly place on jig and slowly tighten clamps.

C - clamp

All 4 pieces may be steamed and bent in one operation if done carefully

Allow the boards to dry thoroughly before removing the clamps.

·4· While the boards are drying whittle or plane the strips for the crosspieces to half round.

·5· On a piece of heavy wrapping paper mark off 2" squares and lay out the shape of the snowshoe including toe and harness holes. If one half is drawn carefully and cut out, and then folded along the center line, the other half may be cut exactly the same. The holes for the lacing of the crosspieces may also be located on the pattern and indicated on the boards with a punch or awl.

2 inch squares

Toe Hole

·6· Lay two of the boards together and place the pattern on them. Fasten it with a few thumb tacks. Mark the outline around the outside and toe hole.

If the harness and lacing holes are marked on the pattern, indicate them as mentioned in 5. [Note - If a few splinters loosen up where the boards are bent, trim them off with a sharp plane.

·7· Cut boards to shape with a band saw, jig saw, or hand saw, or if needs be, a jackknife will do the trick. Cut toe holes.

·8· If the lacing is to be done with rawhide, soak it in water for from 6 to 10 hours before using. Lay cross pieces in place and draw pencil lines on boards to show exactly where holes are to be placed. Use ⅛" bit or drill and bore holes close to pencil lines.

Or, if soft copper wire is to be used, drill holes just large enough for wire to pass thru easily and drill them on the lines.

Wire about ³⁄₆₄" thick is just right for this purpose.

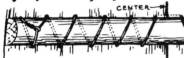

·9· Lay crosspieces in place and fasten with a few small brads from below to keep them in place while being laced.

·10· Lace as tightly as possible and fasten wire end by twisting and hammering down.

·11· There are 4 places where the boards are fastened together. Wire these also.

·12· Round off all edges and bore 2 holes ⅜" in diameter as shown, for harness fastening.

·13· Apply a coat of boiled linseed oil and when that has dried, apply one or two coats of spar or floor varnish.

· SNOWSHOE HARNESS ·

Below is shown a simple harness that may be made of soft buckskin or rope. Dotted line shows where toe of shoe should be when harness is fastened.

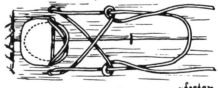

fasten ends with knot

When walking with snowshoes the toes of the shoes or mocassins go thru the toe holes as shown below, thus keeping the snowshoes from slipping backwards. The forward end or toe of the snowshoe is lifted and the heel is dragged along. Keep them in a dry place.

207

ALASKAN ESKIMO SNOWSHOES

It took about an hour to go into the woods, find and cut four elm saplings, trim one set down with a drawknife, and bend them ready for drying as shown on the plate in Figure 6. The other two were laid in the creek with some stones to hold them down. This was done to keep them pliable, so that they could be fashioned a week or so later. Green wood bends very nicely, but don't try to do all of the bending in one operation; it must be worked little by little. In snowshoes for men, it would probably be well to put cross-lacing in the center webbing, as shown in Figure 4.

The Indians made snowshoes similar to those used by the Eskimos, but they made theirs longer and narrower. They put in five cross-pieces and used very close webbing of fine rawhide lacing or caribou gut. (See Figure 6). Long, narrow snowshoes are used where open, flat country is to be traversed, while the bear-paw type, shown in Figure 5, is used in wooded country and where the going is rough.

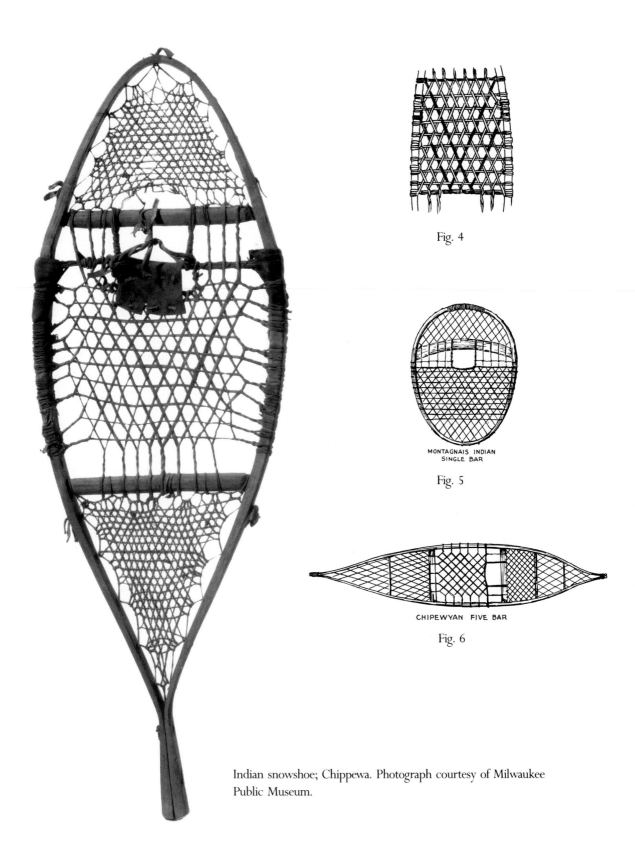

Fig. 4

MONTAGNAIS INDIAN
SINGLE BAR

Fig. 5

CHIPEWYAN FIVE BAR

Fig. 6

Indian snowshoe; Chippewa. Photograph courtesy of Milwaukee
Public Museum.

ALASKAN ESKIMO SNOWSHOES

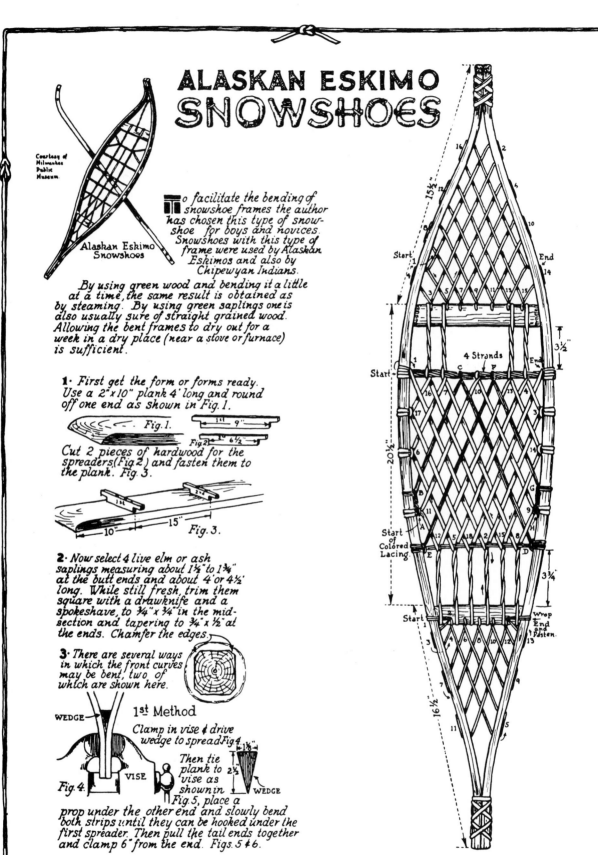

Courtesy of
Milwaukee
Public
Museum.

Alaskan Eskimo
Snowshoes

To facilitate the bending of snowshoe frames the author has chosen this type of snowshoe for boys and novices. Snowshoes with this type of frame were used by Alaskan Eskimos and also by Chipewyan Indians.

By using green wood and bending it a little at a time, the same result is obtained as by steaming. By using green saplings one is also usually sure of straight grained wood. Allowing the bent frames to dry out for a week in a dry place (near a stove or furnace) is sufficient.

1· First get the form or forms ready. Use a 2"x10" plank 4' long and round off one end as shown in Fig. 1.

Fig. 1.

Fig 2.

Cut 2 pieces of hardwood for the spreaders (Fig.2) and fasten them to the plank. Fig. 3.

Fig. 3.

2· Now select 4 live elm or ash saplings measuring about 1½" to 1¾" at the butt ends and about 4' or 4½' long. While still fresh, trim them square with a drawknife and a spokeshave, to ¾" x ¾" in the midsection and tapering to ¾" x ½" at the ends. Chamfer the edges.

3· There are several ways in which the front curves may be bent, two of which are shown here.

1st Method

WEDGE

Clamp in vise & drive wedge to spread Fig.4

Fig. 4.   VISE

Then tie plank to vise as shown in Fig. 5, place a prop under the other end and slowly bend both strips until they can be hooked under the first spreader. Then pull the tail ends together and clamp 6" from the end. Figs. 5 & 6.

WEDGE

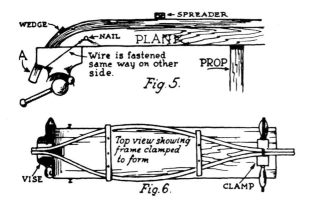

PLANE

WEDGE

←NAIL

A

Wire is fastened same way on other side.

← SPREADER

PROP

Fig. 5.

Top view showing frame clamped to form

VISE

CLAMP

Fig. 6.

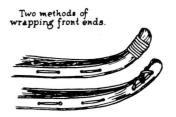

Two methods of wrapping front ends.

2nd Method

If no large vise is handy, make a jig as shown in Fig. 7. Tie or clamp the front ends together and bend in same manner as in 1st Method. Allow a week to dry.

square hole large enough to receive ends.

FRAME

←Clamp   *Fig. 7.*

4. *Before taking frames from forms, mark the locations for the crosspieces (see large drawing). Cut the crosspieces of hardwood and fit them into mortises in frame, cut ¼" to ⅜" deep.*

1⅝"   ¼"

8⅜" to 8¼"
FRONT CROSSPIECE

1¼"   ¼"

6½"
REAR CROSSPIECE

5. *Wrap front end tightly with wet rawhide, set crosspieces into mortises, pull tail ends together and wrap.*

WEBBING

Eskimos use walrus hide and Indians use rawhide for webbing. The snowshoes shown in the upper left hand corner are webbed for crusted snow. If no rawhide is obtainable, use so-called rawhide belt lacing, cut ⅛" wide for the ends and ¼" wide for the middle section. Either type of webbing should be thoroughly soaked before using and put on while wet. The detailed drawing shows the method of webbing. Lace the front & rear sections first. It is advisable to make a tracing of the frame on paper & then lay out the webbing on the paper first. Do not pull rawhide too tight as it may pull the frame out of line when dry. Just pull it moderately tight. About 12 feet of ⅛" lacing is used for the front end and and about 6 feet for the tail end About 28 feet of ¼" is used for the middle.

Be careful to weave over and under uniformly as shown. Webbing at ends is drawn thru ³⁄₁₆" or ¼" holes in frame & crosspieces. Numbers show order of procedure.

For the middle webbing start where indicated & go across & back twice, making 4 strands, then go under & over, & proceed in numerical order, twisting and fastening as shown at left. The darkened strand is then woven in, fastening when shown, and following the alphabetic order as indicated, finally fastening end at H.

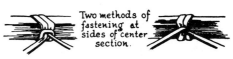

Two methods of fastening at sides of center section.

The darkened strand may be dyed red or green, by putting aniline dye in the soaking water, and will give the snowshoes an added bit of decoration.

When the rawhide has dried thoroughly give the frame & the webbing 2 or 3 coats of good spar varnish.

Note - *The author suggests lacing with heavy cord first to see if everything will work out right. A change in the curve of the frame may mean a change in the webbing also. Make splices as shown.*→

End wrappings.

Splice pulled up tight.

BOW DRILLS

In some of the coast villages where the Eskimos have contact with white men, the breast drill and the "Yankee" drill are very popular with the Eskimos. But wherever there are Eskimos, there is use for a drill of some kind, and the bow drill is still used a great deal. It is important for making holes for rivets or holes for rawhide thong. The Eskimo likes the bow drill, because with it he can apply pressure while drilling. This cannot be done with the pump drill.

DATA OBTAINED FROM
9th ANN. REPORT OF THE
BUREAU OF ETHNOLOGY.

ESKIMO OPERATING A BOW DRILL

Totem pole carved in 1860; Haida, British Columbia. Photograph
courtesy of Milwaukee Public Museum.

A BOW DRILL

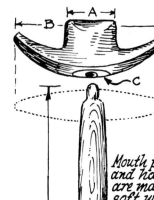

THE MOUTH PIECE
Section A is held between the teeth and is shaped to fit, while the wings, B, are made to fit over the cheeks. Wings are sometimes left off. C is a piece of bone or metal fitted into mouthpiece for shaft to turn in.

Mouth piece and hand piece are made of soft wood.

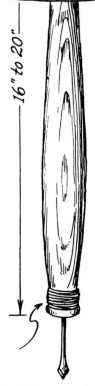

12" to 16"

One turn around shaft.

To operate a bow drill, work the bow back and forth. The point must cut both ways.

To fasten thong

16" to 20"

Bow drills, which also date back a good many years, are still being used. The kind described here are like those used by Eskimos and are easy to make. Used in the Eskimo manner, with a mouth piece, one hand operates the bow while the other holds the material being drilled. When using the hand piece, the material must be held in some other way, as both hands are required to manipulate the drill.

More pressure can be applied with a bow drill than with a pump drill. Eskimos use bow drills for drilling ivory, bone, wood, and even metal.

THE SHAFT may be made of any good wood but it should be perfectly straight and round.

THE BOW should be of hardwood, about an inch wide and 1/4 to 5/16 inch thick. Eskimos frequently ornament their bows with carvings.

THE BOWSTRING can be made of a good leather shoe lace or thong. It gets hard usage.

THE DRILL POINT is made of iron or steel, shaped as shown for pump drill. It is driven into the shaft. Wrap shaft with sinew or wire to keep it from splitting.

HAND PIECE

Hand piece should be about 2½" to 3" in diam. with rounded top and metal or bone socket set into bottom.

CROOKED KNIFE. – made of ivory and an iron blade riveted together.

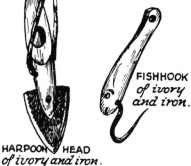

AN ADZ – bone handle, iron blade wrapped with walrus hide.

BONE BELT HOOK.

HARPOON HEAD of ivory and iron.

FISHHOOK of ivory and iron.

LAZY SQUAW COILED BASKETS

The "lazy squaw stitch" does not mean that it is a lazy person's way of making baskets. It is the name given to the simplest method of making baskets. There are many kinds of coiled baskets, some woven of material as fine as heavy thread. These baskets are made of fibers, grasses, and roots, some split and some used as they are found.

The method described has been chosen because of its simplicity. If carefully done, beautiful work will be the result. The materials are also easy to get.

Raffia can sometimes be bought already dyed, but if the desired colors cannot be obtained, it is simple to dye the raffia with any commercial dye. Fiber cord or cane can also be used for the core.

Some types of weaving are very difficult. Coiled baskets of grass and roots are made by Eskimos. In other countries the natives use palm fiber for similar kinds of baskets. The American Indians of the Southwest often use yucca.

Basketry; Hopi. Photograph courtesy of Milwaukee Public Museum.

Lazy Squaw Stitch — Coiled Grass Baskets

The coils of these baskets are made of long-bladed grass such as marsh or sword grass, which should be cut in mid-summer, and carefully laid out in a shady, well ventilated place until thoroughly dry. To use it, first immerse in water until pliable and then lay between wet cloths, from which it is taken as needed. Raffia, which can be bought at florists or basketry supply houses, is moistened the same way. If the material becomes dry while working, dip your hand in water and moisten the materials by running your hand over them. When work is laid aside for the day, hang it up where it can dry or the grass may get moldy. *

*When resuming work on unfinished basket, dip the whole thing in water before starting to work.

1 When both materials are moistened as explained above, take a bunch of grass the thickness of a pencil and start wrapping (at the butt ends) with raffia as shown below. Fig. 1.

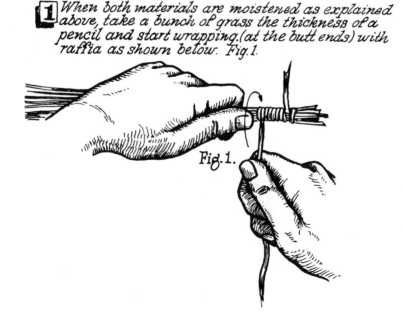

Fig. 1.

2 *Wrap firmly for about 1½ to 2 inches, working it into an arc as shown in Fig. 2.*

Fig. 2.

3 *Twist into a tight coil and sew with a large darning needle as shown in Fig. 3, pulling the raffia as tight as possible. Then wrap around 4 or 5 times and sew it around the previous coil, etc. The ends at "A" are cut off flush.*

Fig. 3.

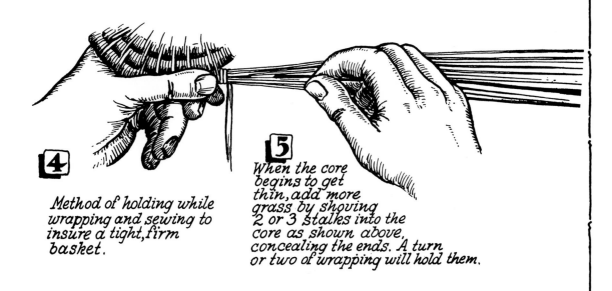

4 *Method of holding while wrapping and sewing to insure a tight, firm basket.*

5 *When the core begins to get thin, add more grass by shoving 2 or 3 stalks into the core as shown above, concealing the ends. A turn or two of wrapping will hold them.*

6 Fig. 4.

When raffia gets too short, pull it thru the core and cut it off, leaving about an inch projecting. Fig. 4.

Start new binder as shown in Fig. 5, letting an inch of it extend. Lay both ends along the core and wrap around them to fasten them.

Fig. 5.

7 Hot pads can be made by coiling flat to the desired dimension, from 5 to 8 inches in diameter. They may be ornamented as shown in second illustration at top of page. This is done with colored raffia. The white raffia is given a couple of turns over the space that the color is to cover. The colored raffia is then wrapped around and the same is done with the end as before

Neither of the binders need be cut for this pattern. For some patterns the ends are secured as in Figs. 4 & 5.

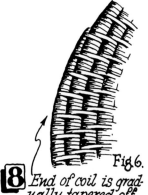

Fig. 6.

8 End of coil is gradually tapered off to make a nice even edge in finishing a pad or basket.

Note: Always keep the raffia winding close together so that it completely covers the grass core.

9 When making a basket, the bottom is made like a hot pad, but instead of a tapered ending, the coil is worked upward to form the sides. Fig.7. The shaping of the basket is a matter of individual taste and is governed by the eye of the worker.

Fig.7.

[Bottoms of deep baskets need not be decorated.]

Colored raffia may be used to ornament baskets. For some designs, the colored raffia will have to be cut, but if possible run it along the core and cover with the white and vice versa. Fig.7. Finish top edge of basket as shown in Fig.6.

10 Ring handles can be made by winding a couple of stalks of grass in a circle and wrapping it with raffia. Fig.8. Sew handles to basket with raffia.

Ring Handle

Fig.8.

11 To make a cover fit snugly, it should have a flange to fit the inside of the basket. Make ring as shown in Fig.8, and sew it to the underside of the cover with raffia.

Cover

Basket

Ring sewed to cover

BIRCH-BARK BASKETS

Paper or canoe birch has always been a boon to
Indians and backwoodsmen. Beautiful and serviceable,
canoes were made from it, and it was used to cover
wigwams, baskets, and pails. Birch is getting scarce,
and the bark should not be peeled from living trees.
But should a tree be blown down, or cut down to
make room for roads or for building houses, it would
be a shame to let the beautiful bark go to waste or be
burned. Baskets and pails made of birch bark will last a
long time, because the wood is resinous and therefore
almost waterproof. The birch-bark basket shown in the
plate opposite was used for collecting maple sap.

Another type of basket which may be used for
gathering berries and the like, is shown in the sketches
in Figures 1 and 2. Figure 1 shows how the bark is cut.
Then the flaps are turned up, after which the ends are
folded around them. In Figure 2, one end is shown
completed and the other end is partly bent in place.
These baskets are not as picturesque as the one on the
opposite page, but they do very well in an emergency,
and they are very useful.

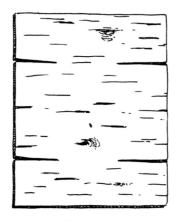

Fig. 1

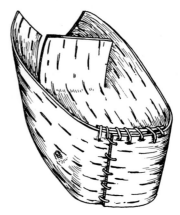

Fig. 2

Birch-bark basket; Woodland. Photograph courtesy of Milwaukee
Public Museum.

BIRCH-BARK BASKET

Baskets like these are used by the Indians for carrying and storing purposes. When used for water or maple sap, the seams are smeared with pitch from pine trees heated and applied while hot. The inner bark is turned to the outside of basket.

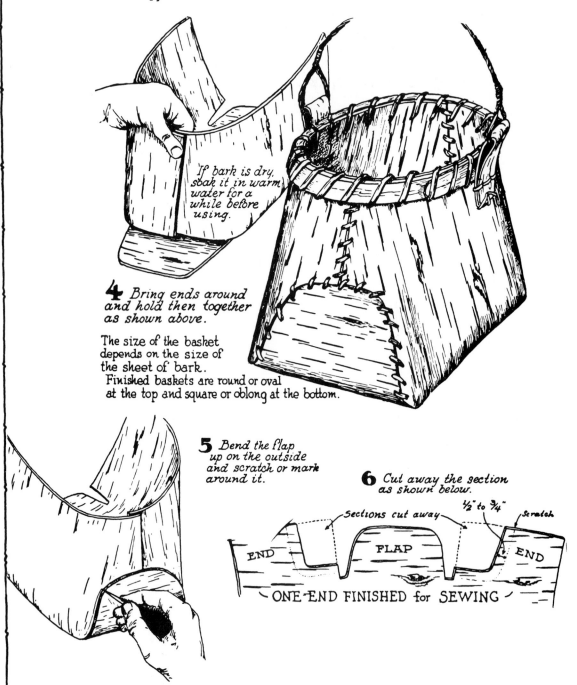

If bark is dry, soak it in warm water for a while before using.

4 Bring ends around and hold then together as shown above.

The size of the basket depends on the size of the sheet of bark.

Finished baskets are round or oval at the top and square or oblong at the bottom.

5 Bend the flap up on the outside and scratch or mark around it.

6 Cut away the section as shown below.

Sections cut away

½" to ¾"

Scratch

END

FLAP

END

~ ONE-END FINISHED for SEWING ~

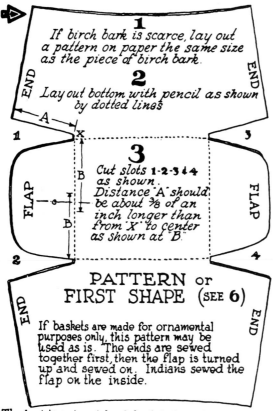

1 If birch bark is scarce, lay out a pattern on paper the same size as the piece of birch bark.

2 Lay out bottom with pencil as shown by dotted lines

END   END

A

1   X   3

FLAP   **3** Cut slots 1-2-3-4 as shown. Distance "A" should be about ⅜ of an inch longer than from "X" to center as shown at "B."   FLAP

B

B

2   4

PATTERN or FIRST SHAPE (SEE **6**)

END   END

If baskets are made for ornamental purposes only, this pattern may be used as is. The ends are sewed together first, then the flap is turned up and sewed on. Indians sewed the flap on the inside.

The best time to get birch bark is in spring or early summer & it should be use while it is still fresh.

Punch holes with awl as you go along.

B

A

7 Turn up flap "A" and bend the ends around and over it. Sew seam "B" first and then sew around flap as shown at center top.

8 Sew with inner basswood bark which should first be well dried and then soaked in water before using, or use wet raffia.

9 After both ends are sewed, level off the top edge with a sharp knife or shears.

10 The top rim band is then whittled out of some green wood ½ to 1 inch wide and from 1/16 to ⅛ inch thick.

11 Sew it to the outside of the bark as shown in the upper center drawing.

Birch bark bale loop

12 Cut two loops of birch bark and sew them on as shown at upper center.

13 Make bale or handle of rope of twisted basswood bark or raffia as the case may be.

14 Seams and cracks may be sealed with pine pitch which should be heated in a small can, and applied to seams while hot. Large cracks should be sewed up before pitch is applied.

Baskets for berry picking should not be pitched.

PACK RACK

Pack frames, pack boards, or pack racks are names which all refer to the same thing. They are used for carrying or packing loads, such as camping equipment, food, or other gear while traveling on foot. A canvas bag or a piece of waterproof material may be used to cover the different sized loads.

It is best to use rawhide in fastening the parts together, because it provides flexibility, and permits the pack to give as the wearer is climbing over rough places. Copper wire may be substituted for the rawhide.

If a pack rack is made of green wood, the joints are likely to loosen when the wood dries. The rawhide bindings should then be soaked by wrapping wet cloths about them. After about 24 hours, the rawhide will have limbered up and may then be stretched tight again. If copper wire has been used, it may be possible to tighten the joints simply by twisting the ends of the wire.

The bands keep the pack from pressing against the wearer's back and provide air circulation beneath the pack.

B — 2" to 2¼"

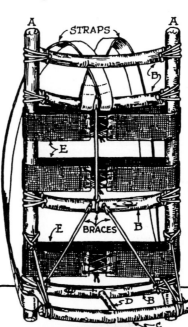

MORTISE AND TENON

SET IN PLACE

AND FASTENED WITH STRIPS OF RAWHIDE.

This frame may be made of green bass wood which is very light and easy to work, or it may be made of ash which, while easy to work, is heavier and more substantial. Where saplings and small trees are plentiful, one may find pieces that have the proper curve, thus saving a lot of time and work, steaming and bending.

Back view of pack rack, arms slip thru straps.

FLAT SIDES

Bend ribs in pairs around two 4½" or 5" logs. If ribs are made of green wood let them dry out thoroughly before removing.
If ribs must be steamed or bent with heat, leave them on the form for a day or two only.
Braces may be made of rawhide or wire.
Dimensions may be altered to suit the wearer. Buckles on the shoulder straps are a convenience.

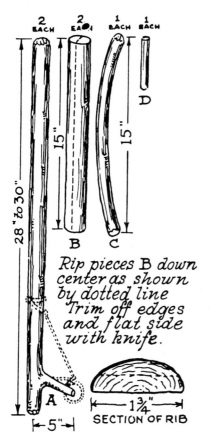

2 EACH
2 EACH
1 EACH
1 EACH

28" to 30"

15"

15"

B

C

D

A

5"

1¾"
SECTION OF RIB

Rip pieces B down center as shown by dotted line. Trim off edges and flat side with knife.

In true woodsman's style all joints are fastened with rawhide. Soak ¼" strips of rawhide for from 12 to 20 hours. Pull it around the joints as tight as possible. When dry the thongs will hold them tightly. Shellac the rawhide to keep out moisture.
Make bands E of 3½" upholstery webbing or heavy canvas.
Fold end over and sew with heavy cord. Open webbing with a pointed stick to insert grommets. In the absence of grommets sew around the holes with heavy cord.
Lace bands tightly

INDIAN LADLES, BOWLS, AND DRINKING CUPS

There are a few project ideas that might be mentioned here: using shallow burls for making ash trays and pin trays.

Wood spoon; Kickapoo. Photograph courtesy of Milwaukee Public Museum.

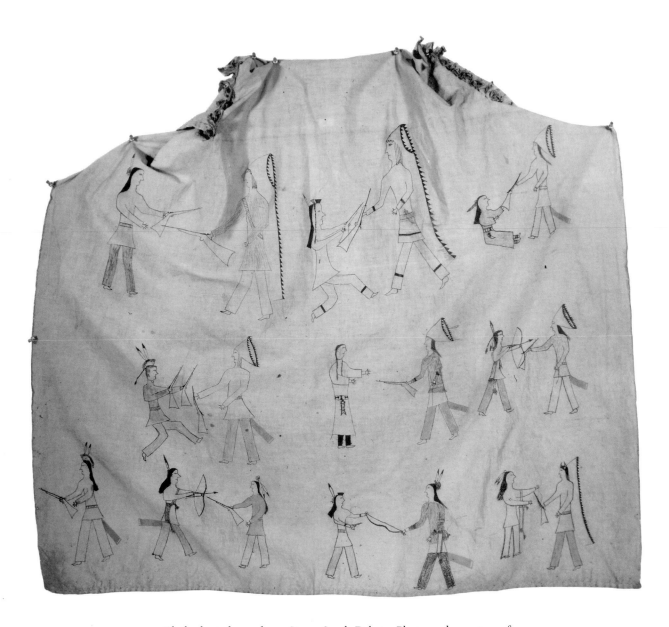

Cloth ghost dance dress; Sioux, South Dakota. Photograph courtesy of
Smithsonian Institution, National Museum of the American Indian.

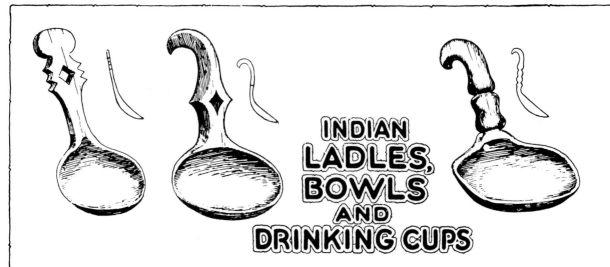

INDIAN LADLES, BOWLS AND DRINKING CUPS

OBLONG BOWL

ROUND BOWL

Indian ladles or spoons vary in size. Some are as small as 3½ inches, while others are from 8 to 10 inches overall. Maple is the ideal wood to make them of but is rather hard to whittle unless they are first roughed out with a saw. Basswood is ideal for whittling and will not crack or check easily.

Burls are found in nearly every woods. It is surprising how many there really are when one is on the lookout for them. They are nature's way of healing a wound in a tree usually caused by a branch breaking off close to the trunk. Take along a sharp saw when hunting burls and saw them off as shown below. Green or live burls are much easier to carve than dead or dried burls.

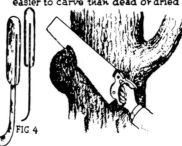

FIG 4

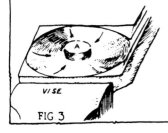

VISE

FIG 3

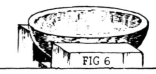

FIG 6

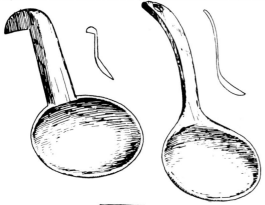

FIG.5

Fig. 5 shows a burl after it has been sawed off. In many instances the center portion contains a partly rotted end of a broken branch. This makes it so much easier. If the bark is quite even, leave it on until the bowl is roughed out If it isn't even, remove it, as there might be a bad spot in the burl itself, which means the wound in the tree hasn't been healed over completely, and the burl will not make a good bowl or cup.

Bowls and drinking cups are usually made from oak or ash burls. They were burned out in some cases and carved out in others A curved knife was used for this purpose, but the work may also be done with a gouge. Bowls measure 6 to 10 inches across, while drinking cups are from 3 to 4 inches in length or diameter, depending on the shape of the vessel.

Fig. 6 shows how the burl may be clamped in a vise while carving When the sides begin to give, take it out of vise.

As burls usually have a somewhat curly grain, a very sharp gouge should be used, gouging out in the same manner as shown in Fig. 3. The thickness of the walls of a large bowl should be about ⅜ or ½ inch and the wall of a drinking cup should be from 3/16 to 1/4 inch.

The only work necessary on the outside of burl bowls or cups is to even up any irregularities and to cut the bottom flat so they can be set down. Fig. 7.
Drinking cups can be shaped like the ones shown above, and a cord or leather thong inserted

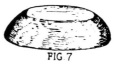

FIG 7

in a hole bored thru the lip. A small crosspiece of wood

is tied to the loose end of the thong and the cup may be hooked or fastened to ones belt while hiking, where it will be handy at all times. Cups and bowls made of burls need not be finished in any way other than smoothing with sand paper.
A spoon gouge is a handy tool for carving out bowls

SPOON GOUGE

Fig. 1 shows a block of wood with the outline of the side view drawn on one side of it. The saw cuts are shown by dotted lines. The block should be held in a vise.

FIG.1

Fig. 2 shows the roughed out blank and the outline of the ladle drawn on the face of it. The bowl of the ladle should be hollowed out at this stage, because it is easier to handle while still in the square. Then if the knife or gouge should slip, the shape can be changed somewhat, whereas if the outside of the bowl is carved first, a slip may ruin the whole thing.

FIG. 2

Fig. 3 shows how the bowl should be carved out. Work toward the center, leaving a small section stand "A", until the proper curve and depth is attained. It serves as a stop, and is cut off when the bowl is finished The rest of the work is just a matter of whittling. Finish up with sandpaper. Then give the ladle as many coats of bacon fat as it will absorb. After that, wash it in hot water and try it out on a good mulligan stew. Of the sketches shown at the top of the page, all but the center ladle were made by Indians. Larger ladles were used for cooking and dishing out foods.

Fig. 4 shows a knife with the end of the blade bent in a curve, for carving out bowls, ladles, etc.

BAG WEAVING

Winnebago bag weaving, as it is often called, is practically a lost art among the Indians today, although the Nez Percé Indians still make a similar bag using twisted corn husks and wool. Among the woodland Indians, however, one sees only the bags that were made years ago. Some of these bags are true works of art.

Using a heavy jute cord for the warp is better than using wool. The jute tends to give the bag more body. In the older bags, the colors are rather subdued, either from use or because they were dyed with vegetable dyes. But with the brightly colored wools of today, very beautiful bags or purses can be made.

Use 1"x 1½" Strips of any soft wood.

These frames can be used for two sizes of bags.

Putting on paint in tepee; Assiniboine. Photograph courtesy of
Milwaukee Public Museum.

THE INDIAN METHOD OF WEAVING.

WOODLAND INDIAN BAG WEAVING

This is the simplest form of finger weaving and was used by Chippewa, Fox, Winnebago, Potawatomi, Menomoni and other Indians living in the forests. They made the threads of the inner bark of basswood or cedar, of milkweed fiber, or of buffalo wool.

A thick jute cord for the warp, and a heavy wool yarn, make a nice combination to work with, or 2 or 3 strands of light wool can be twisted together to make one weft strand. These bags were formerly used as storage bags. Smaller bags of this type can be used for handbags, purses, shopping bags, etc.

◄1► Start off by tying a double cord as shown at left. This will be the bottom of the bag when it is finished.

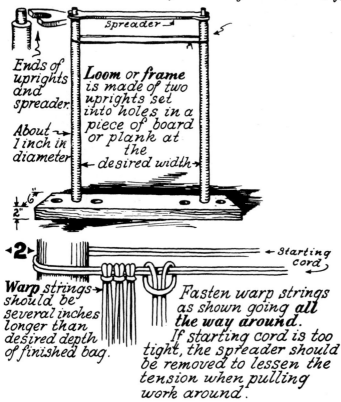

Spreader ►

Ends of uprights and spreader.

About 1 inch in diameter

Loom or frame is made of two uprights set into holes in a piece of board or plank at the desired width►

6"
2"

◄2► ← Starting cord

Warp strings► should be several inches longer than desired depth of finished bag.

Fasten warp strings as shown going **all the way around.**

If starting cord is too tight, the spreader should be removed to lessen the tension when pulling work around.

‹3› *Loop a strand of wool around one pair of warp strings at the left side of loom and start to weave as shown below. Do not pull too tight but keep the work close enough to cover or hide the warp strings. The wool used to weave with is called* **woof** *or* **weft**.

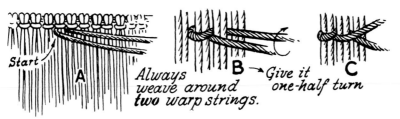

Start

A

Always weave around **two** *warp strings.*

B → *Give it one-half turn*

C

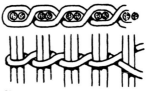

The weaving goes around spirally. New weft strands are knotted to the ends of the old ones and the knots are concealed by putting them to the inside of the bag.

POSITION OF HANDS WHEN WEAVING

With forefingers and thumb reach between the two weft strings XX, and grasp next two warp strings. Warp is then held taut while weft is pulled taut as shown at right. Weft may be twisted left or right, but should be consistent all the way around. Handle warp with left hand & weft with right hand.

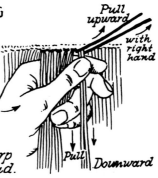

Pull upward

with right hand

Pull *Downward*

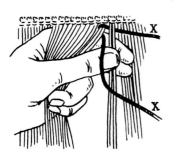

X

X

Different colors are always started and finished at the same warp threads.

Plain twist *weaving, using only one color of weft.*

Twined *work, made by dividing the warp strings at each round of weaving.*

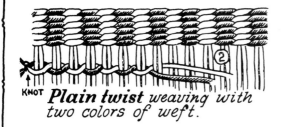

Plain twist *weaving with two colors of weft.*

KNOT

Twined *work with two colors of weft.*

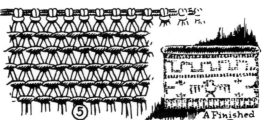

A Finished Bag

Loose twined *work like this may be made by using fishnet cord for both warp and weft. Different colors may be used but no designs are used.*

Top view showing how **concealed twist** *is woven. This process makes it possible to weave different patterns*

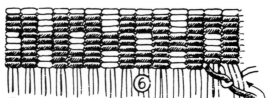

Give the weft strings a full twist when concealing one color and only a half twist when alternating.

A variety of patterns can be worked out by using the methods shown above. A bag can be made up of a series of different colored bands or of wide bands, each worked out with different patterns and colors. The twist can also be reversed for variety.

◄4► The beginning of the bag is the bottom of the finished bag, and sewing it up is the last operation.

To finish the top of the bag, take it off the frame and put it back upside-down. The loose ends of warp are then sort of rolled into a rope and wrapped by sewing (Fig. 1 at right), or with a closely sewed button hole stitch Fig. 2. Often the edge is bound with a strip of colored cloth. Fig. 3.

◄5► If a zipper is to be sewed onto the opening, the ends may simply be finished by knotting one warp string of one pair to one of the next, etc, going completely around twice. Sew zipper to this edge.

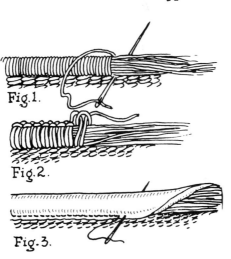

Fig. 1.

Fig. 2.

Fig. 3.

A loop handle.

A few simple patterns for repeat borders and the method of laying them out

TURTLE SHELLS

Cleaning out the inside of a turtle shell seems to be quite a job, but if you live in the country or are at camp it is quite simple. Clean most of the flesh out of the turtle shell, then lay it on top of an ant hill. The ants, in return for the food you have brought to their door, will clean out every bit of flesh and in a few days you will find the shell as clean as a whistle.

When setting a box turtle shell on an ant hill, be sure to tie the flaps shut, then bore the holes for the stick. The ants can then go in and out of the holes to do the cleaning up.

Old Bear, a medicine man (Mandan), George Catlin, 1832. Photograph
courtesy of Smithsonian Institution, National Museum of the American
Indian.

OTHER USES FOR TURTLE SHELLS

IROQUOIS RATTLE.

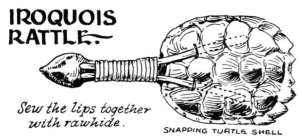

Sew the lips together with rawhide.

SNAPPING TURTLE SHELL

Making an Iroquois rattle is almost a taxidermy job, but is worth the trouble. First cut off the legs and tail, leaving enough skin for sewing up the openings. Clean out the insides thru these openings with a long, thin knife. Cut away as much meat as possible from the neck bones but leave the bones in. Cut out tongue. Now wash every part with hot water, sling out as much water as possible and hang up for a half hour or so. Then dust the inside thoroughly with powdered alum. Get enough on. Then before the skin dries, sew up the tail and leg openings with thin rawhide lacing. Tie a cord loosely around the neck, just back of the head, stretch out the neck, & let it hang until thoroughly dry. Cutting the holes in the shell for the sticks will let air circulate in the inside and hasten the drying. When dry, cut flat hickory strips as shown, drop some shot or pebbles into shell, insert ends of sticks, (note dotted lines) and fasten by wrapping with strips of flat basswood bark. A 7 inch shell make a nice sized rattle.

NECKERCHIEF SLIDES -

MADE FROM A 2 INCH SHELL

Baby turtles have very thin, soft shells, so take it easy with your knife.

can be made from common mud turtles. Clean out the shell nicely and sprinkle inside with powdered alum. Then insert a smooth stick about the size of the ordinary slide opening & let the shell dry on it. Otherwise the shell might shrink or curl too much.

BOX TURTLE RATTLE

WHITTLED STICK

WRAP PROJECTING
END OF STICK WITH
LEATHER OR CORD TO
HOLD IT IN PLACE.

SIDE VIEW OF
BOX TURTLE RATTLE.

FRONT - SHOWING
WHERE END OF STICK
COMES THROUGH.

Box turtle rattles are very easy to make. Clean out the inside of the turtle very carefully, wash out with hot water and sprinkle thoroughly with powdered alum. Then drill holes, as shown, with a pocket knife, and whittle the handle. Put stones or shot into the shell and close it up. These shells close up completely. Push the stick thru the holes and tie some cord or leather around the end projecting thru the front part of the lower shell as shown and your rattle is ready to dry. The handle can be painted or covered with red cloth.

LEG RATTLES

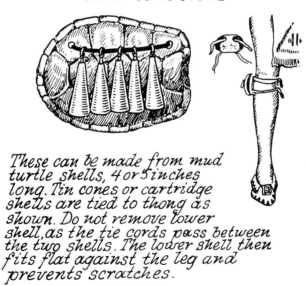

These can be made from mud turtle shells, 4 or 5 inches long. Tin cones or cartridge shells are tied to thong as shown. Do not remove lower shell, as the tie cords pass between the two shells. The lower shell then fits flat against the leg and prevents scratches.

FLAGEOLET OR LOVE FLUTE

Flageolets, or love flutes, have been mentioned by every chronicler of Indian lore since Coronado; they were not copied from the settlers. It seems logical that they were first made in countries where cane or bamboo grew, as these are the materials which are easiest to shape and adapt for these instruments. Even in northern countries, bamboo flageolets and whistles are often seen.

Any of the woods mentioned in the plate on page 244 may be used to make a love flute, although cedar somehow seems to look the best. Making a love flute is not as difficult as it may seem, but the wood must be straight grained, and the chisel and plane must be sharp.

The flageolet shown in the photograph has a very sweet, low tone. Because the holes are equally spaced, the notes are perfectly scaled. Three overnotes can be played on the cedar flageolet and two on the bamboo, making it possible to play popular tunes that use one octave.

In the old days, love flutes were used at night only, by the young brave who wanted to serenade his sweetheart. After hearing the soft, low notes, one can readily understand how a dozen or more of these flutes could be played in the same camp without interfering with each other.

Flageolets were not used in ceremonies. They are also called buckskin flutes, probably from the fact that they are usually wrapped with buckskin to keep them from splitting or opening up at the glue joint. Single-toned shrill whistles made of eagle-wing bones are used by the Indians in the Sun Dance. These were also used in the past for signalling and directing warriors during a battle.

Frank James playing love flute, 1941; Chippewa. Photograph courtesy of Milwaukee Public Museum.

INDIAN FLAGEOLET
OR LOVE FLUTE

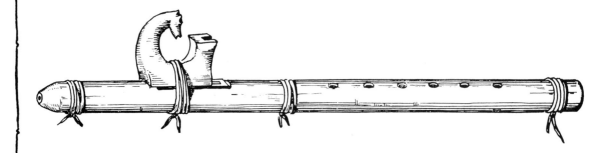

There are few white folks today who have heard the soft, low-pitched notes of an Indian love flute. It is seldom played in the daytime and is not used for dances or any other celebrations. As the name implies, it is used by the love-sick young warrior to serenade his lady friend after the sun has set and everything is quiet around the camp. Of those examined at the Milwaukee Museum, two were made of cedar and one was made of bamboo. The author has made flutes of both of these woods which have very sweet tones, and also one of white pine which has a pleasing tone.

HOW TO MAKE ONE OF CEDAR OR WHITE PINE

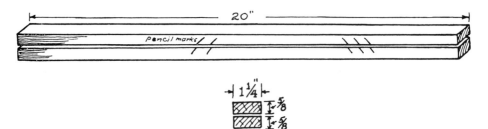

·1· Get a piece of straight grained wood 1¼ inches thick, and carefully rip off two ⅝ inch pieces. Mark as shown, to insure same position. If carefully sawn, the two pieces will fit perfectly for gluing.

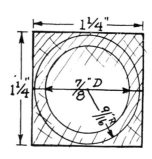

·2· Place both pieces together, find center at cut, and with a compass or dividers, mark one end as shown at left. On the other end, (the mouth-piece) mark the outer circle only. The flute when finished should be 1³⁄₁₆ inches in diameter. Leaving the pencil mark stand will give you that dimension.

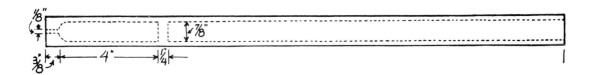

·3· On inner surface of each half, mark as shown above, using a marking gauge if one is handy. A knife cut will do also.

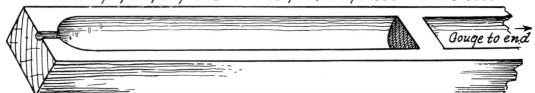

·4· Each half is then gouged out with a ½ inch inside-bevel gouge. By fitting a long handle to the gouge, you will find it much easier to cut out the longer ends, which are 15¼ inches long.

It is a good idea to make a template as shown to insure a nice round hole when the two halves are placed together When using sandpaper to finish the inside, use a ½ inch dowel for a sanding block.

·5· *To lay out openings and holes proceed as shown below.*

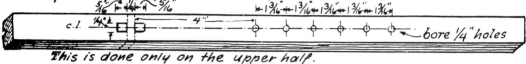

c.l.

bore 1/4" holes

This is done only on the upper half.

·6·
Cutting

Looking from above

Lip

This cutting can be done best with the small blade of a pocket knife.

Lip

Looking at inside of top piece

Section of upper half.

Section of lower half.

·7· *Now wait — don't glue the halves together until you know it will work right. First make a little jigger as shown at the left. (block) Hardwood is best but soft wood will do. We use cherry wood for these.*

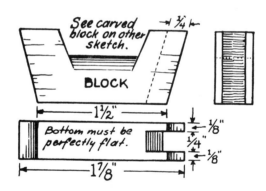

See carved block on other sketch.

3/4

BLOCK

1 1/2"

Bottom must be perfectly flat.

1/8"
1/4"
1/8"

1 7/8"

·8· *Then, from some 1/32" material such as lead, celluloid, fiber, or even cardboard, cut a piece as show below.*

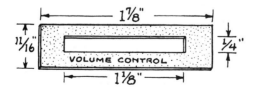

1 7/8"

11/16"

1/4"

VOLUME CONTROL

1 1/8"

·9· *Now place the halves of the flute together and tie by wrapping securely with cord.*

·10· *Place volume control over holes as shown at right and place the block over the volume control in about the position shown below.   Tie block in place as shown in illustration at top of other plate.*

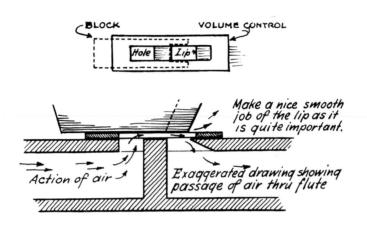

BLOCK   VOLUME CONTROL

Hole | Lip•

Make a nice smooth job of the lip as it is quite important.

Action of air →

Exaggerated drawing showing passage of air thru flute

·11· *You will have to shift these two pieces back and forth to find the proper tone setting. When you know you have everything shipshape, take off wrappings, glue the halves together and wrap securely. Let the glue dry thoroughly.*

·12· *Round carefully, leaving the part under the block & vol. control flat. The Indians cut down at this place as shown in sketch. If this is done it should be cut down before the lip is cut.*

·13· *To finish, give the flute a few coats of linseed oil and wrap with buckskin as shown in sketch. Try carving a fancy hardwood block.*

TO MAKE A FLAGEOLET OF BAMBOO

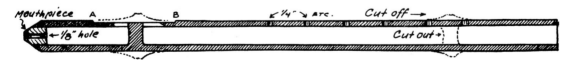

Mouthpiece   A   B   ←¼"→ ATC.   Cut off →

←⅛" hole   Cut out →

Get a piece that corresponds to the dimensions given for the cedar flute. Cut out one of the inner walls with a 9/16" bit and a ½" gouge. Cut flat section for block, A-B, and cut the holes on either side of the other wall. Carefully fit mouth piece and drill ⅛" hole thru as shown. Glue mouthpiece in place. These are easy to make but should be well wrapped to prevent splitting.

INDIAN TOM-TOM

The tom-tom plays an important part in the life of the Indian. It is used by many different tribes the world over. The one described is made of thin rawhide.

Indians make tom-toms using but one face of rawhide and tying it as shown in Figure 1. Then there is the deep-voiced tom-tom made of a hollowed section of log, such as may be found in almost any woods. Cut a section about 12 inches long off a 12- to 14-inch hollow log. Cut away all the rotted inner wood, take off the bark, and smooth the outside surface. Next, round the outer edges, and stretch the rawhide over both ends. After this has dried, decorate both the tom-tom heads and the wood that shows between the thongs (see Figure 2).

An old iron kettle with three legs also makes a good drum. The handle should be removed and the rawhide stretched as shown in Figure 3, passing the thongs around the kettle legs.

The drumstick shown in Figure 4 is made by wrapping cord or leather around a straight stick.

For dance purposes, the tom-tom is usually suspended by thongs from three stakes as shown in Figure 5.

Fig. 1. Back of a single-faced tom-tom.

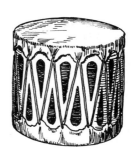
Fig. 2

Fig. 3

Dream Dance drum; Woodland. Milwaukee
Public Museum.

Fig. 4

Fig. 5

HOW TO MAKE AN INDIAN TOM-TOM

The rawhide used should be less than 1/16" thick.

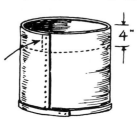

4"

Cut two disks of thin rawhide two inches larger in diameter than the wooden frame and punch holes about two inches apart and one-half inch from edge. Punch them evenly so they will match up as shown in lower left sketch.

Do all cutting of rawhide while it (the rawhide) is dry.

Loop of raw hide passed thru holes and knotted on inside

Cut 4" strip from top of cheese box and cut thru outer piece where indicated with arrow. Remove tacks, then pull together to 12" in diameter and fasten with clamps. Bore holes and lace with wet rawhide and let dry, or fasten with tacks clinched on the inner side. Paint red or brown.

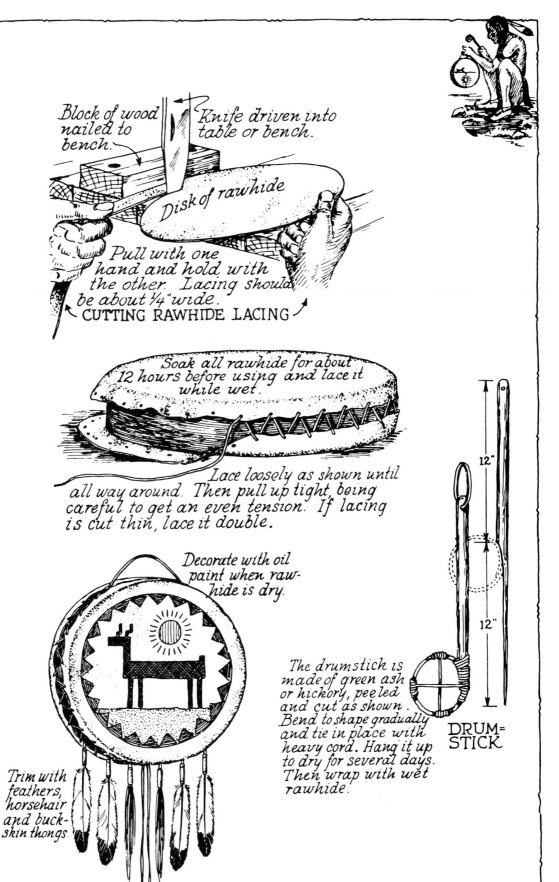

Block of wood nailed to bench.

Knife driven into table or bench.

Disk of rawhide

Pull with one hand and hold with the other. Lacing should be about ¼" wide.

CUTTING RAWHIDE LACING

Soak all rawhide for about 12 hours before using and lace it while wet.

Lace loosely as shown until all way around. Then pull up tight, being careful to get an even tension. If lacing is cut thin, lace it double.

Decorate with oil paint when rawhide is dry.

Trim with feathers, horsehair and buckskin thongs.

The drumstick is made of green ash or hickory, peeled and cut as shown. Bend to shape gradually and tie in place with heavy cord. Hang it up to dry for several days. Then wrap with wet rawhide.

12"

12"

DRUM=STICK

INDIAN GOURD RATTLES

An Indian ceremonial dance with the tom-toms, rattles, and sleigh bells all sounding in perfect unision, the colorful headdresses and costumes of the dancers, is something that once seen will be remembered for a long time.

The gourds must be started in a cold frame or hothouse. When the weather is warm enough they must be set out, preferably along a south wall.

If no gourds are obtainable, rattles can be made of thin rawhide. To do this, cut rawhide to the shape shown in Figure 6. After soaking the hide in water, sew it as shown in Figure 7, leaving the ends loose. Turn the head thus formed inside out and fill it with sand. Tie up the ends and let the rawhide dry out thoroughly. Next, cut a handle as shown in Figure 8. Then empty the sand out of the rawhide head, and soften the ends in water until they are pliable. Place two or three stones inside the head and tie it to the handle as shown in Figure 9. Decorate the rattle with paint and give the rawhide a coat or two of varnish.

Grass dance costume; Plains. Photograph courtesy of Milwaukee Public Museum.

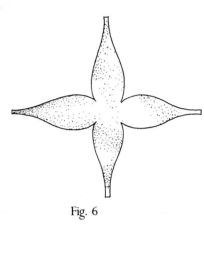

Fig. 6

Fig. 7

Fig. 8

Fig. 9

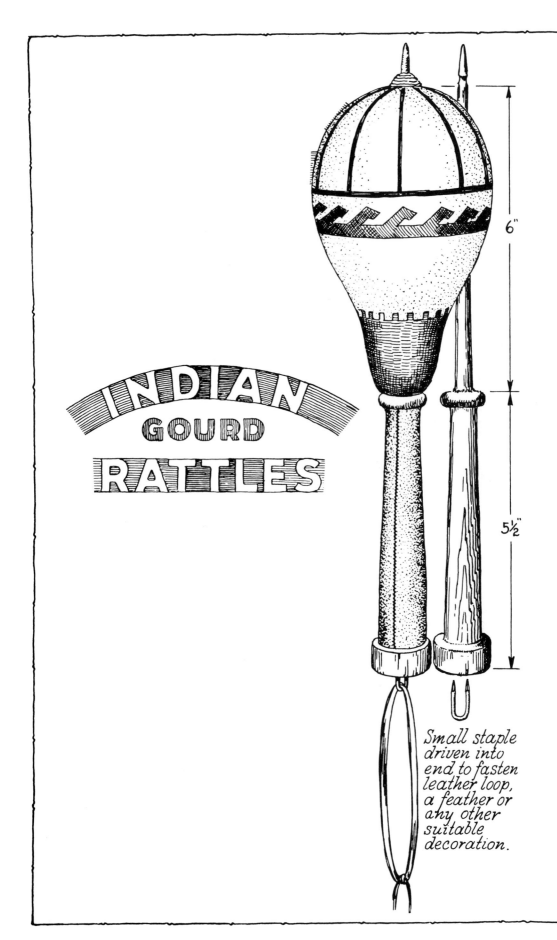

INDIAN GOURD RATTLES

6"

5½"

Small staple driven into end to fasten leather loop, a feather or any other suitable decoration.

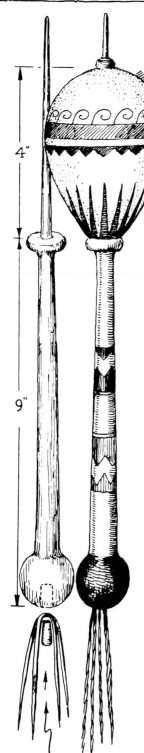

4"

9"

A quarter-inch
hole drilled in end
of handle, into
which a wooden
plug is driven to
fasten a few thin
strips of buckskin

Rattles made almost as much
of the dance music of the
American Indian as the
tom-tom. They were made of turtle
shells, rawhide and gourds.
While easier to obtain, gourds are
also more adaptable to ornamentation
The gourd at the left is commonly
called the nest egg gourd, and as it is
pure white when dried, it is ideal for
decorating with paint. They are from
3 to 4 inches long.
The gourd at the right is the common
green-striped variety which dries out
to a light yellow. A coat of cream or
white-colored paint may be applied,
and the designs or symbols painted
on over that.
Cut a hole in each end to fit the stick.
Take out the dried seeds thru the larger hole,
and put in 5 or 6 round stones about
1/4" in diameter. Then insert the stick
and fasten it at the upper end by
wrapping a thin strip of leather or cord
set in glue around the stick until a
knob is formed. The handles may
be painted with suit-
able designs. The orig-
inal of the one at the
left was covered with
beads while the one to
the right was covered
with buckskin.

Plant some mixed gourd
seed early in spring and
have dried gourds by
New Years.

Note: Any dry wood may be
used for the handle and be sure
the gourds are perfectly dry
before using them.
Don't forget to put in the stones
or BB shot before fastening the
stick. Seeds can be loosened with
a piece of wire.

255

BEADED·ARM·BANDS

This one is made of tubular beads with leather spacers to keep the rows in place.

TUBULAR BEAD

LEATHER SPACER

After one row of beads is strung, try it on the arm to see if it fits properly. Use waxed linen thread.

X

First cut this arm band out of a piece of soft leather, leaving ends long enough for tying.

The beads can be sewed directly onto the leather as shown at X, or they can be woven on a bead loom and sewed onto the leather later. Unless leather is very thin, use an awl.

FEATHER·ARM·ORNAMENTS

LEATHER DISK

SOFT LEATHER BAND

TIN DISK

Finished ornament to be about 5" in diameter

-**1**- *Cut a 2½ or 3-inch disk of rawhide or sole leather*
-**2**- *Soak it in water and form it into a saucerlike shape. Let it dry this way.*
-**3**- *Punch holes and fasten loops for leather band.*
-**4**- *Large feathers are now sewed all the way around. A drop of cement will hold them until then. A second row of small fluffs are next fastened in the same manner, with a drop of cement and one stitch.*
-**5**- *A small tin disk is then tied over the center. Disk may also be fastened to a wide elastic arm band.*

SLEIGH·BELL·LEG·BANDS

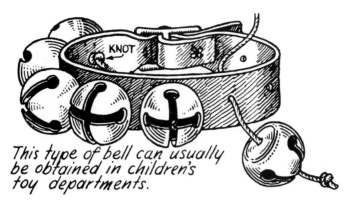

This type of bell can usually be obtained in children's toy departments.

Sleigh bells form an important part of most of the Indian dances. Their rhythmical jingling coupled with the steady beat of the tom-tom is enough to stir the blood of anyone. The drawing shows how these bands are usually made, although they may be fastened in any simple manner.
These bands are worn tight below the knee or loosely at the ankle.

TIN·CONE·ANKLE·BANDS

These cone anklets emit a very pleasant tinkling sound, especially if enough cones are used. There should be about 30 or 40 on each band. They can be fastened to the buckskin thong as shown below or by crimping with a nippers

These patterns are actual size. Tin, brass or copper may be used.

Use long cones on one and short ones on the other

Cones can be shaped over the end of a center punch.

PACKSADDLES

In areas where packing is part of the day's work, packsaddles can be bought at trading posts; but in other places, they are rarely seen. Pack horses are most efficient for hauling camp equipment and food through woods and rough country.

It is really not very difficult to make a packsaddle. Be sure to fit it to the horse for which it is intended, and see that the pads are placed properly. Put a good thick blanket under the saddle and see that the weight of the load is properly distributed on the horse's back.

In very rough hilly country, two bellybands are sometimes used, besides the breast and breeching straps.

Dimensions shown on these plates are for Indian ponies. For horses the cross arms should be 18 inches long and pads may be made somewhat longer also.

Inasmuch as packsaddles usually get a lot of rough handling, and carry dead weight, the crossbars should be of some fairly hard wood, such as oak or ash. Pad boards can be of some softer wood.

Cut out 4 pieces as shown below with a snug fitting half-lap joint. The cross pieces fit together at right angles, and are fastened with a ¼" rivet or carriage bolt. Round off all edges and corners.

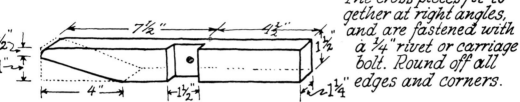

When using rivets have them project ⅛" beyond the washer, (1) and hammer them down tight (2).

If carriage bolts are used, be sure to drive the square shank into the wood before tightening the nut.

Holes should be ¼ inch. The joints must be snug fitting or the packsaddle will soon become a wobbly affair.

These dimensions will do for the average horse or large pony.

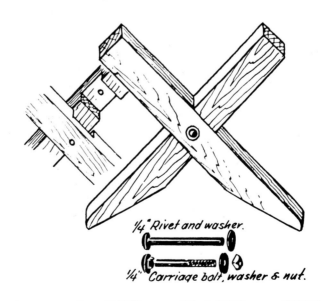

¼" Rivet and washer.

¼" Carriage bolt, washer & nut.

PACKSADDLES

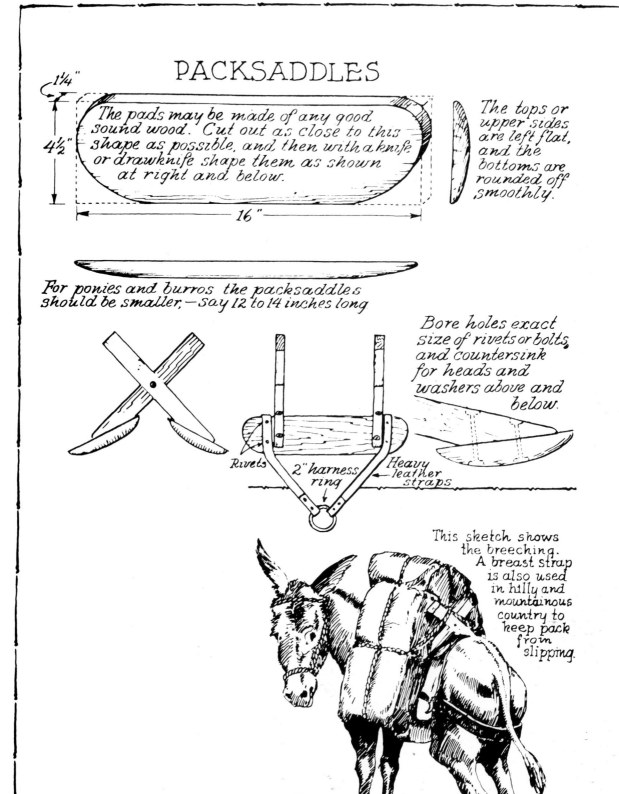

1¼"

4½"

The pads may be made of any good sound wood. Cut out as close to this shape as possible, and then with a knife or drawknife shape them as shown at right and below.

16"

The tops or upper sides are left flat, and the bottoms are rounded off smoothly.

For ponies and burros the packsaddles should be smaller,—say 12 to 14 inches long

Bore holes exact size of rivets or bolts, and countersink for heads and washers above and below.

Rivets
2" harness ring
Heavy leather straps

This sketch shows the breeching. A breast strap is also used in hilly and mountainous country to keep pack from slipping.

A PIONEER PACKSADDLE

Saplings should be of hard wood such as oak, ash, hickory or maple. Pads may be of soft wood.

X

2" Saplings
Rawhide Slabs

In a pinch, a good serviceable packsaddle can be made with saplings, slabs and rawhide. Measurements and straps are the same as the one described above and on opposite page.

❶ Whittle or saw half way thru the saplings and trim out as shown at left, to make as snug a fit as possible. ❷ Make the slant cuts and cut ¼" deep grooves where rawhide lashings are to come. ❸ Bind together with wet rawhide at X. (above) ❹ Place bucks on pads, mark and bore or burn holes.

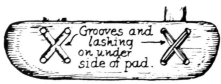

Grooves and lashing on under side of pad.

❺ Cut grooves in bottom of pad for rawhide to lay in. The grooves should be deep enough to bring lashings below the surface of the pad.
❻ Then lash securely with wet rawhide thongs. When these have dried you will have a pretty tough packsaddle.
Be sure you have enough padding under the packsaddle and see that the bellyband is alway tight. Adios.

DOG HARNESSES

The dog harnesses shown on the plate are
the ones commonly used. If, however, one should wish
to use a dog for pulling a cart or wagon, two special
items must be made. The first is a pair of loops, one
on each side of the bellyband where it crosses the
traces. These loops should be only large enough to fit
the shafts of the vehicle. Then, there should be longer
traces and a method of fastening them to the
whiffletree. The latter may usually be done by cutting
a slot in the trace as shown in the upper sketch on the
plate of dog harnesses.

When hitching up several dogs to form a team, they
are placed one ahead of the other and the traces are
tied to the sides of the dog behind. The Eskimo
method of hitching the dogs abreast of one another in
fan shape is only used in open country where there are
no trees or shrubs. In deep snow, one man on
snowshoes usually breaks trail, and dogs and sled
follow in the same track. Another man handles the
sled and the two change places when the trail breaker
gets tired.

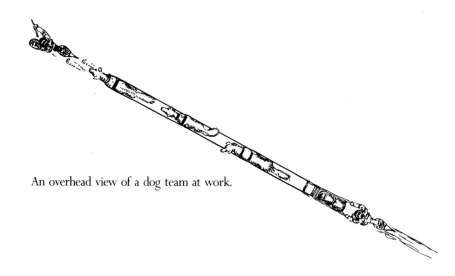

An overhead view of a dog team at work.

Man in costume on horseback, Spotted Rabbit; Crow, Montana. Photo
by Fred R. Meyer, 1903–1910, courtesy of Smithsonian Institution,
National Museum of the American Indian.

DOG HARNESSES

Any of the larger sized dogs can be trained to haul a sled, a cart or a travois, or to carry a pack; and if he is not overloaded, he will enjoy a hike with his master in spite of the fact that he is harnessed. But care should be taken not to overload him. Give him a load he can pull easily and help him pull when the going is tough

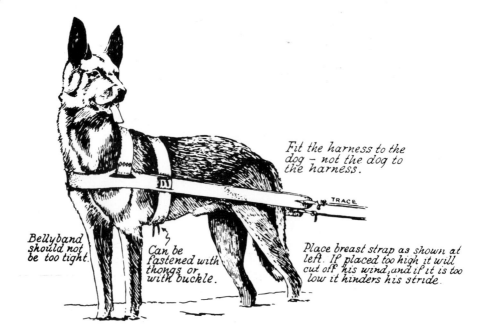

Fit the harness to the dog – not the dog to the harness.

Bellyband should not be too tight.

Can be fastened with thongs or with buckle.

Place breast strap as shown at left. If placed too high it will cut off his wind, and if it is too low it hinders his stride.

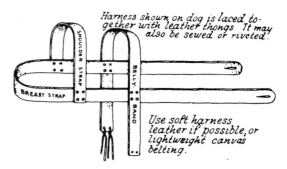

Harness shown on dog is laced together with leather thongs. It may also be sewed or riveted.

Use soft harness leather if possible, or lightweight canvas belting.

Harness straps should be from 1½ to 2 inches wide depending on the size of the dog.

HARNESS FOR SLED OR TOBOGGAN

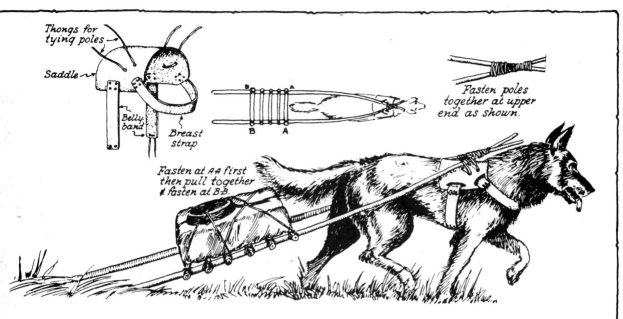

Thongs for tying poles

Saddle

Belly band

Breast strap

Fasten at A-A first then pull together & fasten at B-B.

Fasten poles together at upper end as shown.

Make the saddle of some thick, soft leather or of 2 or 3 pieces of canvas sewed together and bound on the outer edge.

The breast strap & belly band for a canvas saddle should be sewed or riveted on. With a leather saddle they may be fastened thru slits as shown above.

HARNESS FOR DRAG OR TRAVOIS

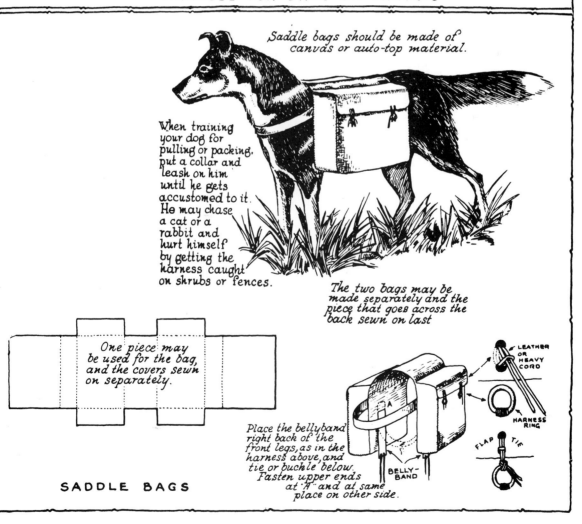

Saddle bags should be made of canvas or auto-top material.

When training your dog for pulling or packing, put a collar and leash on him until he gets accustomed to it. He may chase a cat or a rabbit and hurt himself by getting the harness caught on shrubs or fences.

The two bags may be made separately and the piece that goes across the back sewn on last

One piece may be used for the bag, and the covers sewn on separately.

LEATHER OR HEAVY CORD

HARNESS RING

FLAP TIE

Place the belly band right back of the front legs, as in the harness above, and tie or buckle below. Fasten upper ends at "A" and at same place on other side.

BELLY-BAND

SADDLE BAGS

INDIAN TEPEE

Beyond a doubt, the tepee is a comfortable all-around tent—its only drawback is carrying the poles. Where it is set up for a vacation camp, it can be made very comfortable in all kinds of weather. And one of its chief assets is that it allows the campers to light a fire and cook in it in bad weather. The smoke flaps are set to draw the smoke out of the tepee and everything is lovely.

If the poles are all of equal length, a piece of canvas may be set over the ends to keep out a heavy rain, lifted into place with a pole, and fastened by cords at three or four places.

The canvas should not hang down too far, or it may interfere with the smoke draft. In warm weather, the lower edge of the tepee can be lifted up and plenty of ventilation may be had.

The radius used for the tepee shown on the opposite page is 10 feet. The smoke flaps extend 12 inches.

With the rain cover in working order

Indian and tepee at Ft. Belknap Reservation; Plains. Photograph
courtesy of Milwaukee Public Museum.

INDIAN TEPEE

Tepees may be made of 8 or 10 oz. canvas depending on what they are to be used for. If it is to be used for camping, 10 oz. would be best. The dimensions given are for a 10' tepee which will accommodate 4 or 5. If a larger one is wanted, increase the radius and make the smoke opening larger to accommodate more poles. Canvas comes in different widths but the strips are laid as shown and should be double sewed. All edges are hemmed to prevent fraying. Poles should be straight and about 12' long. Peel off the bark and trim off some of the wood from the butt ends to lighten them. Poles should be smooth to prevent tearing the canvas.

About 12 poles are required for a 10' tepee. Poles measuring 2" at the butt and 1" at the tip are about right.

When laying out the two edges that are to be laced together, be sure that the door openings and the pin holes are equally spaced on each side

The easiest way to decorate a tepee is to spread it out on a level place. Lay out the designs with a pencil and paint with ordinary house paint thinned down with turpentine. Red, yellow, blue and black are the colors most commonly used.

A ring of 5" or 6" stones about 2' in diameter in the center of the tepee forms the fire place. Do not burn wood with a lot of rosin or pitch as it will soon blacken the inside of the tepee. While a little discoloration from smoke gives the tent a used appearance, too much makes it a messy thing to handle or live in.

By carefully folding, this tepee can be rolled into a bundle 2½' to 3' long by about 10" or 12" in diameter. It should be kept in some sort of bag or covering to prevent wearing at the edges and to keep it clean.

Keep poles in a dry place.

POCKETS

A
Tie loop or cord here.

14"

12"

18"

3½'–4"

2' 3"

1'6"

1'

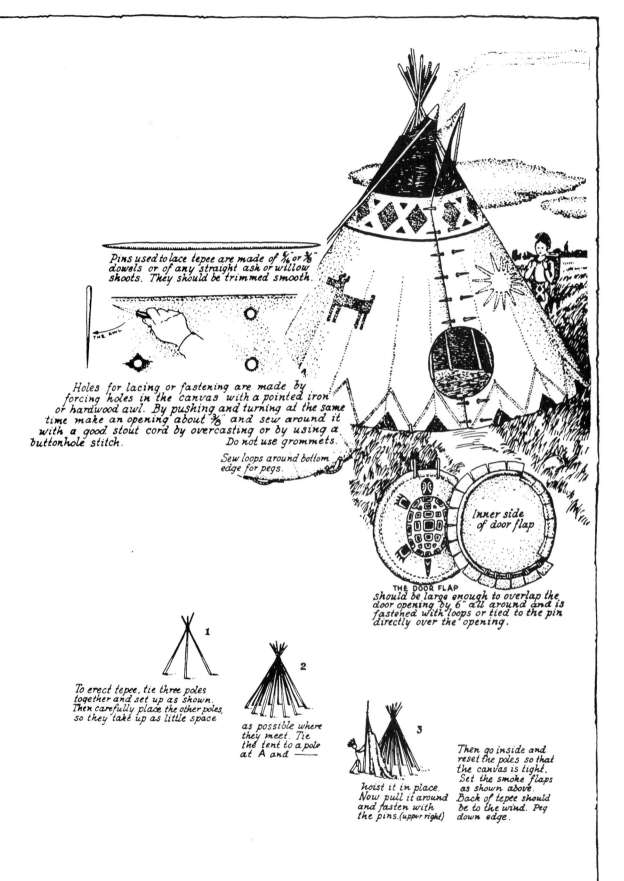

Pins used to lace tepee are made of $\frac{5}{16}$ or $\frac{3}{8}$" dowels or of any straight ash or willow shoots. They should be trimmed smooth.

THE AWL

Holes for lacing or fastening are made by forcing holes in the canvas with a pointed iron or hardwood awl. By pushing and turning at the same time make an opening about $\frac{3}{8}$" and sew around it with a good stout cord by overcasting or by using a buttonhole stitch.   Do not use grommets.

Sew loops around bottom edge for pegs.

Inner side of door flap

THE DOOR FLAP
should be large enough to overlap the door opening by 6" all around and is fastened with loops or tied to the pin directly over the opening.

1

To erect tepee, tie three poles together and set up as shown. Then carefully place the other poles so they take up as little space

2

as possible where they meet. Tie the tent to a pole at A and ——

3

hoist it in place. Now pull it around and fasten with the pins. (upper right)

Then go inside and reset the poles so that the canvas is tight. Set the smoke flaps as shown above. Back of tepee should be to the wind. Peg down edge.

269

INDIAN WIGWAMS

The type of Indian dwelling shown on the opposite page has been in use long before the Pilgrims landed on our shores. In many respects, it is superior to the tepee. Its one disadvantage is that it cannot be taken down and set up in some other spot. It will make an excellent camp shack for a group that has a place where the frame may be left standing through the winter. Even in winter, the snow may be shoveled and swept off the floor space, the frame covered with canvas, and a fire started. In a surprisingly short while, a cozy and warm camp will be ready.

A cover for the smoke hole that can be quickly shifted or closed may be made as shown in the sketch in Figure 1. This canvas must be large enough to overlap the opening about 1 foot on all sides. Large stones are tied to the ends; and by pulling one way or the other, the smoke may be let out, or the hole closed up completely.

Camp; Apache. Photograph courtesy of Smithsonian Institution,
National Museum of the American Indian.

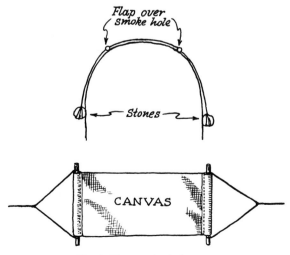

Fig. 1. The smoke-hole cover.

Indians in the North Central States still make this type of wigwam for summer use and for camping. These wigwams may be covered with birch bark or rush mats but in most cases canvas is used. The top or roof is always of some material that is waterproof.

When the summer season is over, the covering is stripped off and the frame is left standing until the next summer. Then with a few minor repairs and a little tightening up it is ready for another season.

Sometimes these wigwams are built round but they are usually built as shown at the right.

The size, of course, depends on the amount of material on hand and the number of boys. 7'x9' to 8'x12' and from 6' to 7' high is a nice size for boys to build.

The mitä'wi'kiöps or medicine lodges of the Menomini Indians of 50 years ago were 60' to 70' long, 20' wide and about 8' high at the center top. They were built in the same manner as the wigwam but the upright poles were about 3" thick at the butt ends.

INDIAN WIGWAM

Floor plan.
Leave space for a doorway at each end.

Below is shown a frame in the process of construction. Make the splices at least a foot long.

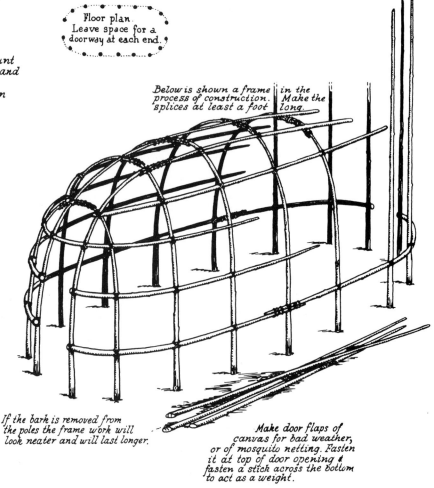

If the bark is removed from the poles the frame work will look neater and will last longer.

Make door flaps of canvas for bad weather, or of mosquito netting. Fasten it at top of door opening & fasten a stick across the bottom to act as a weight.

272

Green saplings of any kind may be used. They should be about 10' to 12' long and not too thick. About 1½" at the butt end is a good size.

Lay out the shape on the ground and set the butt ends about a foot in the ground. Space them about 1½ to 2 feet apart. The ends are then bent down toward the center and bound with whatever you have on hand, thin rope, heavy cord or as the modern Indian does today, with bale wire. Years ago they used strips of inner basswood bark.

The cross poles may be somewhat thinner, about 1" at the butt. Always fasten the butt end of a pole first and then bend and work toward the smaller end.

The upper sketch shows how the wigwam is covered with small pieces and strips of canvas or other material. It may be pinned together with large thorns or with 6 penny nails. Leave an opening in the center of the roof for the smoke hole.

Build the fireplace in the middle of the wigwam by setting stones halfway into the ground in a rectangle measuring about 18"x 24". Then pack clay around the inside, against the stones, making a sort of pan-shaped affair.

In bad weather, the fireplace is used for cooking and in the summer time it is used for mosquito smudges. The stones around the fireplace will tend to keep the ashes where they rightly belong.

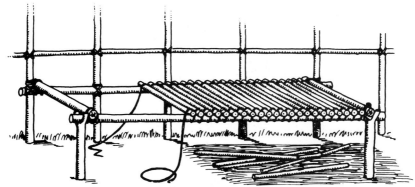

Bunks like this should be built along each side of the wigwam, to serve as beds, places to sit, and for storage space. A layer of pine boughs or hay should be laid over the sticks first and blankets or burlap thrown over that. Use 2" poles for the frame and ½" to ¾" sticks for the cross pieces. Tie them as shown. Do not try to nail them as the frame poles will split and the entire top of the bunk will be loose.

CROOKED KNIFE AND SKEW KNIFE

The white man with his fast-cutting emery and Carborundum wheels can easily grind down files to convert them into knives. The Indian and Eskimo, however, have to do their grinding on a piece of flat stone. When they grind down a file, the file cuts are usually very much in evidence. They just grind the sides of the sharp file until they are fairly smooth, then keep on grinding until a sharp cutting edge has been produced. The large crooked knife shown here (1) is an old Chippewa knife. It was presented to the author by Chief Gogeweosh. The file cuts show up very distinctly on the blade. The blade is 5¾ inches long. This is a rather large knife of its kind. The hole for the tang of the file was burned into the horn and then molted lead was poured in to hold it tight.

The smaller knife (2) was made by the author from a small spike horn; but, instead of burning the hole, it was first drilled and then cut away to fit the tang.

After the lead is poured into the hole, it should be tamped down with a flat punch and a hammer. This method is simpler than the one shown on the plate, provided one has deer horns to cut up. The Chippewas sometimes set the blade into the handle as shown in Figure 2, and then bound it with rawhide. When this is done, the tang of the file must be forged as shown in the sketch. A small crooked knife is a handy tool to have around. It is to the whittler what a gouge is to the carver.

Nothing more need be said about the skew knife (4) except that the handle can be made in halves, one half being cut out to fit the tang, after which the two halves of the handle must be wrapped firmly with rawhide.

Indians and Eskimos prefer to get steel from common carpenter's saws, because this, while being tough and holding an edge quite well, can be cut with a chisel and sharpened and shaped with a file. With care, it can also be bent to the proper shape. Holes can also be drilled into the saw steel.

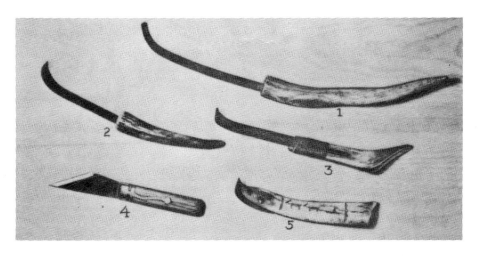

1. An old Chippewa crooked knife with a deer horn handle (from Frank Smart). 2. A crooked knife with a spike horn handle. 3. and 4. A crooked and a skew knife made according to the plates. 5. An Eskimo crooked knife with an antler handle.

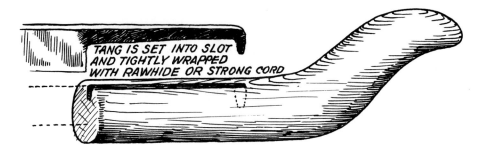

TANG IS SET INTO SLOT AND TIGHTLY WRAPPED WITH RAWHIDE OR STRONG CORD

Fig. 2

INDIAN CROOKED KNIFE

Usual method of holding a crooked knife. The cutting is done toward the worker.

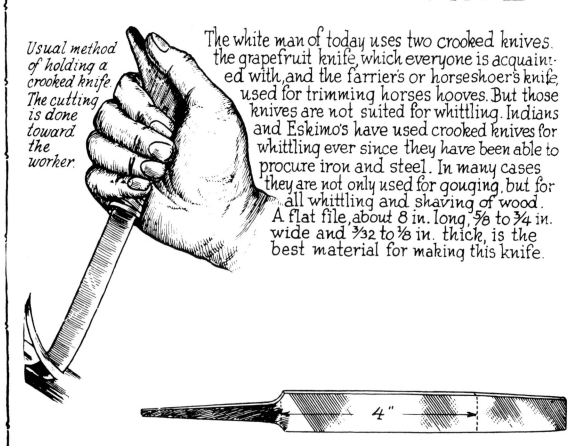

The white man of today uses two crooked knives. the grapefruit knife, which everyone is acquainted with, and the farrier's or horseshoer's knife, used for trimming horses hooves. But those knives are not suited for whittling. Indians and Eskimo's have used crooked knives for whittling ever since they have been able to procure iron and steel. In many cases they are not only used for gouging, but for all whittling and shaving of wood. A flat file, about 8 in. long, 5⁄8 to 3⁄4 in. wide and 3⁄32 to 1⁄8 in. thick, is the best material for making this knife.

· 1· Grind the file down until no file cuts show. Use emery wheel.
· 2· Then break off the end, leaving 4 inches of flat surface.
· 3· Now grind cutting edge on one edge. (Indians sometimes ground the upper side only ◄— and sometimes both sides.) Grinding both sides will make it better for gouging. ◄— *Fig. 1.*

Fig. 1.

4"

·4· Heat to cherry red and bend blade over round piece of iron,

or over the horn of an anvil to about the curve shown.

cutting edge →

back

Knife blade ready for bending. (For right hand.)

·5· Bend end of tang in the opposite direction.

·6· The blade should now be tempered. This is a job which should be done by one who knows how. (The blade is tempered "glass hard" first and then the temper is drawn by heating to a yellow or straw color.)

·7· We now come to the handle. Let's make it in true Indian fashion. Get a piece of wood 4 inches long by 1½ by ⅝ inches, or a piece of limb as shown. Fig. 2. Whittle it as shown in Fig. 3.

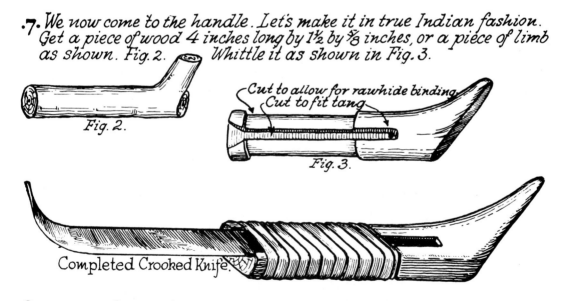

Fig. 2.

Cut to allow for rawhide binding
Cut to fit tang

Fig. 3.

Completed Crooked Knife.

·8· Now wrap handle firmly with wet rawhide as shown and let it dry. Or if no rawhide is to be had, wrap with trolling line or some other good cord, and give the entire handle several coats of boiled linseed oil.

A SKEW KNIFE

This type of knife comes
in handy in many ways.
It can be used for skiving
leather as well as for cutting
and whittling wood. It is rather
easy to make, and requires no tempering.
But it must be ground carefully so as
not to "burn" the metal, which takes the
temper out of it. The metal used is a
worn out power hack-saw blade which
can usually be obtained from some machine
shop. Do not heat this metal as it cannot be
tempered properly again.

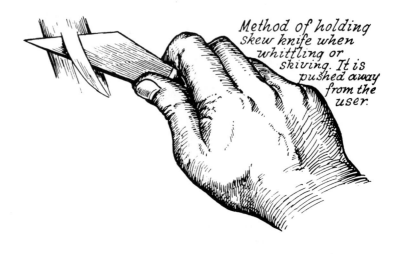

*Method of holding
skew knife when
whittling or
skiving. It is
pushed away
from the
user.*

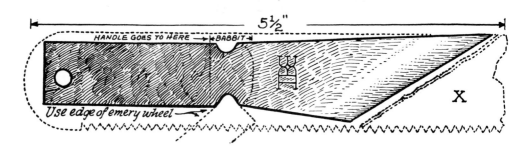

5½"

HANDLE GOES TO HERE → ←BABBIT→

Use edge of emery wheel ←

X

·1· With a colored pencil, lay out the pattern as shown, with a 30° slant for the cutting edge. **·2·** Section X may be broken off by clamping the other part in a vise at that angle and hitting X a sharp blow with a hammer. **·3·** Then grind to shape on an emery wheel.

$3\frac{1}{4}$

$\frac{9}{16}$"

Fig. 1.

·4· Grind cutting edge to a long taper. Be careful not to burn the edge.

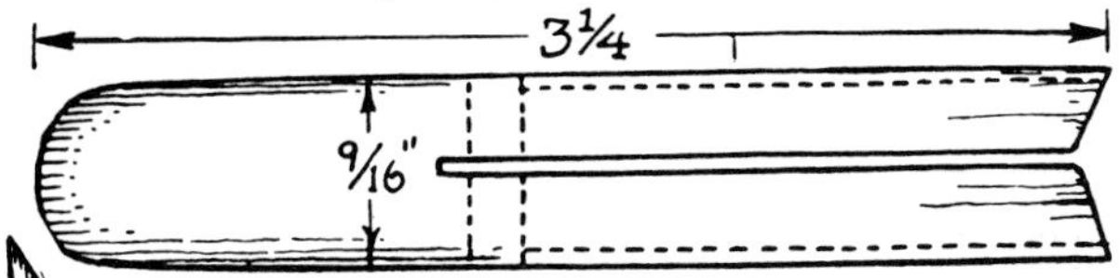

·5· Make handle of any hard wood. Fig. 1. Undercut the grooves

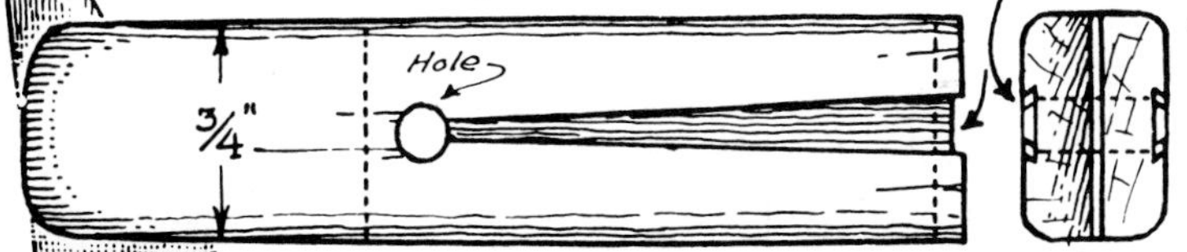

Hole

$\frac{3}{4}$"

END OF HANDLE

PAPER POUR

Paper wrapping should cover hole and project $\frac{1}{2}$ inch beyond edge of wood handle. Fig. 2

·6· Get some pewter or babbit scraps and melt them. In the meantime set blade in handle and wrap with several thicknesses of good wrapping paper, as shown at left, and tie with cord.

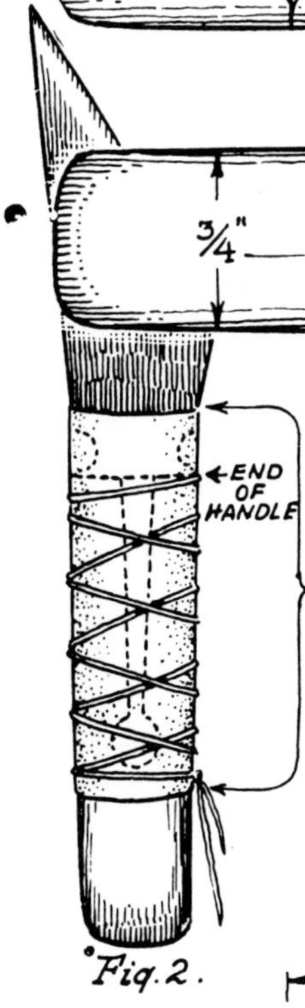

·7· Pour melted metal into cup from both sides until it is filled. Metal will run down groove and into hole.

·8· When cool take off paper and finish with file and emery cloth.

Fig. 2.

$6\frac{1}{2}$"

Completed Skew Knife.

To really finish the job right, a good sheath of leather or wood should be made for this knife.

FIRES

Under certain conditions, it may be difficult to experiment with the actual fires shown. When starting these fires, (or any other fires for that matter), every obvious precaution should be taken. In order to prevent unnecessary danger to yourself or your surroundings, remember the fire safety tips.

Keep your fire under control by maintaining a low flame, using timber of a reasonable size. Be sure to put out your flame completely before leaving your site. Common sense is your best weapon against forest fires.

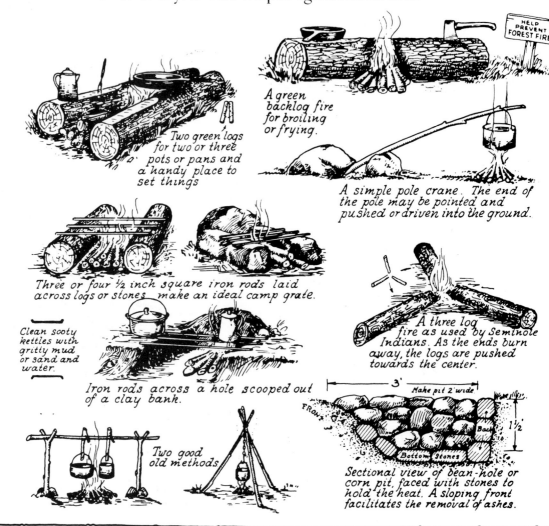

HELP PREVENT FOREST FIRES

Two green logs for two or three pots or pans and a handy place to set things

A green backlog fire for broiling or frying.

A simple pole crane. The end of the pole may be pointed and pushed or driven into the ground.

Three or four ½ inch square iron rods laid across logs or stones make an ideal camp grate.

Clean sooty kettles with gritty mud or sand and water.

Iron rods across a hole scooped out of a clay bank.

A three log fire as used by Seminole Indians. As the ends burn away, the logs are pushed towards the center.

Two good old methods

Make pit 2' wide

3'

1½

Back

Bottom Stones

Sectional view of bean-hole or corn pit, faced with stones to hold the heat. A sloping front facilitates the removal of ashes.

A simple pot-hook.

FIRES

A thin flat stone supported by stones, with a small fire under it makes an excellent warming plate to keep food warm.

A three stone fire. See that pan rests evenly before starting fire.

A two stone fire can be used for more than one kettle or pan.

Don't build fires close to live trees. It may injure or kill them.

Don't build fires against dead trees or logs. It may start a fire that you can't put out.

Don't have dry grass or rubbish near a fire. It may start a grass or forest fire.

Don't leave a fire unattended. Always put it out when you go away.

Don't try to build a fire with green wood. After a rain, remember that "high wood is dry wood".

Don't carry loose matches in your pockets. Keep them in a small bottle well corked or in a waterproof match safe. Dry matches are worth more to you in wet weather than in dry weather.

Don't build a large fire for cooking, unless it's to get embers to bake beans or roast corn.

And Remember- soft wood and small branches for a quick fire & hardwood and knots for a hot fire.

If your camp is near a cut bank, a permanent fireplace may be built like this. A piece of sheet iron makes a better top than stone

Stones

Make the chimney hole first. You may have to try some other place if you strike a large stone or root.

Place stones around top of chimney.

HELP PREVENT FOREST FIRES

A one stone fire. See that pot rests evenly & firmly.

Always hang cooking kettles up off of ground

Cut sides of vent and bend inwards

A safe stove for tepee or wigwam.

Do not cut thru rim.

Opening may be closed to hold fire.

A dandy stove can be made from an old powder can or galvanized pail. Clay banked around the base helps to hold the heat.

CAMP KNIFE

The knife described on the opposite page is just one of many types of hunting and camp knives that you can make. The shape may be changed to suit individual tastes. Care should be taken, in grinding saw blades, that the temper is not taken out of them. Keep a pail or can of water near, and cool the blade every now and then. These saw blades cannot be retempered like other steel. If the knife is made of tool steel, it may be forged and ground to shape after which it must be hardened and tempered.

One may be fortunate enough to find what looks like a long flint "spear head." This, in reality, may be a flint knife. By putting a handle on it, he will have a real Indian ceremonial knife. Flint knives of this kind

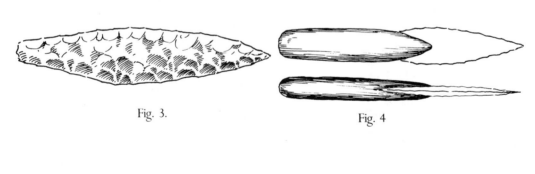

Fig. 3.   Fig. 4

Fig. 5

Fig. 6

Fig. 7

are similar in shape to the one shown in Figure 3 and are from 3 to 5 inches long. Cut a piece of wood to fit it snugly as shown in Figure 4. Then soak some thin rawhide or sinew in water, and after setting the flint into the handle with a good coating of fish glue or, still better, a packing of plastic wood, wrap the rawhide or sinew tightly about it as shown in Figure 5. Another type of flint knife, shaped like the one shown in Figure 6, was used by the Indians without a handle. These knives, when freshly chipped, have a wonderful cutting edge. They vary in length from about 2 to 4 inches. Figure 7 shows how these knives were held while in use.

Knife sheath of deerskin, quilled decoration and knife; Athapascan, Northwest Canada. Photo by Carmelo Guadagno, courtesy of Smithsonian Institution, National Museum of the American Indian.

CAMP KNIFE

① *Use piece of hack-saw blade 1¼" wide. Make a template of wood or cardboard the shape of the desired knife blade.*

Beaded Buckskin Sheath

Tooled Leather Sheath

② *Mark off shape of template on the saw blade with a colored pencil. Break saw blade to desired length by clamping knife part in a vise and striking the projecting part a sharp blow with a hammer. Then grind groove with edge of emery wheel on both sides of blade at A,A, and at B,B, and break off triangular pieces as described above.*

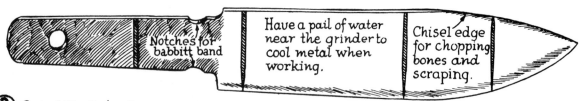

Notches for babbitt band

Have a pail of water near the grinder to cool metal when working.

Chisel edge for chopping bones and scraping.

③ *Grind blade to shape on emery wheel. Wear goggles while grinding. Do not burn steel. When it turns blue or brown it is too late. Taper sides of blade as is shown in the sections on a sanding disk faced with emery, carborundum or garnet cloth. Polish the blade by laying it flat on a piece of wood and rubbing it with emery cloth, using plenty of oil.*

④ *Guard made of ³⁄₃₂" brass. Cut slot to fit snugly.*

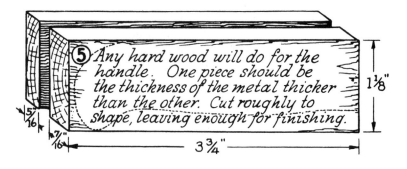

⑤ *Any hard wood will do for the handle. One piece should be the thickness of the metal thicker than the other. Cut roughly to shape, leaving enough for finishing.*

1⅛"

⁵⁄₁₆

⁷⁄₁₆

3¾"

⑥ Slip guard into place and lay tang on the thicker half of handle. Draw line around it and with a knife and chisel carve out so that the tang fits in flush. Then cut away forward end as shown at C. This forms the groove for the babbitt.

This cut may be left out as it is there only for decoration

C

7/8"

⑦ Locate and bore rivet hole in carved half of handle. Clamp other half in place and bore that using first hole as guide.

⑧ Give each half of handle a coat of cold solder or metallic cement. Put blade between two halves of handle and clamp the whole until it is dry.

⑨ Use a copper or brass rivet in handle

View of knife before wrapping with paper to dotted lines.

FINISHED

⑩ Now take a strip of heavy wrapping paper and wrap it around handle, being careful to have it fit snug at the guard and around the wood. Fasten the end with glue. Then carefully cut a hole thru the paper just large enough to pour babbitt thru. Melt hard babbit in small ladle. Warm the knife at this section and pour babbitt. After babbitt has cooled, finish entire handle with file and sandpaper. Use oil, shellac, or varnish as a final finish.

GLOSSARY OF SIOUX NAMES
FOR ARTICLES IN THIS BOOK

The following Sioux names for some of the articles described in this book have been translated by Chief Wanblee Isnala (Lone Eagle) especially for the author. These words are in the Lakota dialect used by the Oglala Sioux. All Sioux understand the Lakota language.

	Lakota	Pronunciation
Arm bands	Hant Kunza	hunt koo za
Arrows	Wau hiukpi	wa-heeu kpee
Baskets	Ciuh tiu	cheeu-tee
Beads	Psi to	pshee-toe
Beadwork	Wak su pi	wak-shu-pee
Birch bark	Taupa ha	tumpa-ha
Bone	Hu hu	hoo-hoo
Bow	Ita zipa	eeta-zee-pah
Breastplate	Wa na piu	wah-nah-pee
Breechclout	Ceg na kee	cheg-nah-kee
Buckskin	Ta ha	tah-hah
Carve	Ba go	bah go
Cherry	Can pa	chau pah
Coup stick	Wa hu Keza	wahoo kee zah
Crooked knife	Mila skopa	meelah shko pa
Feathers	Wi ya ka	wee yah kah
Flageolet	Ciyo tauka	cheeyo taukah
Ghost	Ogle wa na gi	oh-glee wah nah gee
Green tree	Caute ca	chau cha
Hoop	Cau gle ska	chau-glee-shkah
Lacrosse sticks	Tapica psice	top-eecha pseecha
Lance	Wa hu keza	wahoo-kee-zah
Leggings	Huu ska	hoo-ska
Masks	E te ha	ee tay hah
Medicine	Pe zu ta	pej ui tah
Moccasins	Hau pa	hum pa
Peace pipe	Ca nu pa	cha-nu-pah
Pump drill	Wag mu Iyuh loke	wah-gmu eeyu khlokay
Rattle	Rhla rhla	rlah-rhla
Rawhide	Ta ha saka	tah-hah shah-kah
Roach	Pe sa	pey-shah
Saddle	Can waqin	chan wah queen
Shield	Wa ha chanka	wah ha chunka
Shirt	Oglee	oh glee
Snowshoes	Pso hau pi	psoe hum pee
Stitch	Ba se sa	bah she sha
Tepee	Tipi or Ti-ikceya	tee-eek-cheya
Throwing arrows (Crow)	Wau hinkpe ihpeya so loka	wa heenk-pee eekh-pay a sho-lokah
Tom-tom	Ca ce ga	chum-chey-ghah
Turtle	Ke ya	kee yah
Vest	Ogle ptecila	oglee pa tech illa
War bonnet	Wa pa ha	wah-pah-hah
War club	Iyan ka pem ni	eeya ka pem nee
Wood	Can	chahn

INDEX